TERRY ATKINSON

Follow Your Heart

10 FUN-TO-MAKE QUILTS YOU'LL LOVE

Follow Your Heart:
10 Fun-to-Make Quilts You'll Love
© 2019 by Terry Atkinson

For questions or concerns regarding editorial content,
contact: www.atkinsondesigns.com
https://www.facebook.com/atkinsondesigns
instagram.com/atkinsondesigns
pinterest.com/terryatkinson33/

DISTRIBUTOR
To order copies of this book for wholesale, retail,
or individual sale, contact:

Martingale
19021 120th Ave. NE, Suite 102
Bothell, WA 98011-9511 USA
ShopMartingale.com

ISBN 978-1-68356-009-8

Printed in China
24 23 22 21 20 19   8 7 6 5 4 3 2 1

CREDITS
Publisher Atkinson Designs
Distributor/Wholesaler Martingale
Machine Quilting Deb Oscarson, Big Lake, MN
    Shannon Wright, Springfield, MO
Photographer Brent Kane
Book Designer Angie Haupert Hoogensen
Illustrators Terry Atkinson and Elizabeth Tisinger Beese
Technical Editor Elizabeth Tisinger Beese
Copy Editor Durby Peterson

SPECIAL THANKS
Thanks to all of our pattern testers for great
feedback and to the shops that hosted test classes:
The Quilt Sampler in Springfield, Missouri, Calico
Hutch in Hayward, Minnesota, Gruber's in Waite Park,
Minnesota, and All in Stitches in Zumbrota, Minnesota.
Thanks also to Greta Anderson, Rita Kroening, and Linda
Louder for your careful attention to detail and helpful
suggestions.

Contents

Introduction

L ast winter, my husband, Kirk, and I packed up our camper and left Minnesota to spend six months exploring the (warmer!) United States. Along the way, we visited small towns, wilderness, and bustling cities (I even took a side trip to Hawaii!). There is so much to see! Whether it was a quiet cove, a mountain pass, or a rowdy rodeo, everywhere I looked I found inspiration. In this book you'll find the projects that followed.

As always, I'll share my best tips and tricks for making each project as enjoyable as the place that inspired it.

Kirk and I have made our way across most of the southern half of the United States. We have met so many interesting people, seen incredible sights, and eaten lots of local foods. I never realized how much exploring a new area centers around the food! We made a point of seeking out local favorites, be it Tex-Mex, shrimp and grits, BBQ, or coastal seafood, and we loved trying it all.

I'm a Midwestern girl, but I've come to love the beauty of the mountains and the ocean. In all my earlier road trips, I didn't know there was much to see outside of my car. Little did I know! Get out and look around; it's spectacular.

In all of our travels I haven't found a favorite place yet; I've just found places I want to go back and visit again! In fact, we loved our travels so much, we're heading out again this year. I am looking forward to the inspiration that will bring. But in the meantime, take a trip with me and let's start sewing!

Terry

General Information

Every good road guide has a legend that explains the details. Consider these pages your quilting legend with information about the patterns that follow.

Quilt Sizes

The sampler quilt is a lap-size quilt. The other quilts have multiple sizes.

What Are the Numbers in Parentheses?

Example: *(baby, lap, twin, queen, king)* (7, 8, 10, 11, 14)

The numbers in parentheses are for the different quilt sizes. Take a moment to go through and circle the numbers for the size you are making. As you sew, use the circled numbers and ignore the rest!

For example, if you are making the lap-size quilt, circle and use the second number.

Fabric

Yardage is based on 42" width fabric. Fat quarters are 18" × 21". Steam press all fabric before you begin. Prewashing is not recommended for fat quarters because the edges will ravel.

Cutting

Instructions given are for rotary cutting. Measurements include ¼" seam allowance. Cut strips across the width of the fabric.

Fat Quarters: Straighten the fabric edge and cut strips perpendicular to the selvage (finished edge). Strips will be about 21" long.

Yardage: Straighten the fabric edge and cut strips across the width of the fabric from selvage to selvage. Strips will be about 42" long.

Subcut: Turn the strips and square the end. Crosscut these pieces from the strips.

What Rulers Do I Need?

Basic Rulers: Use your favorite rulers for cutting strips and squaring up the blocks. Here are my favorites:

• 8½" × 12½" for cutting strips
• 6½" × 6½" for cutting and trimming small squares
• 12½" × 12½" for squaring blocks
• 6½" × 24" for trimming large sections of the quilt

How to cut triangles: All three of these triangle tools are used in the same way for cutting.

1. First triangle: Align the blunt corner of the tool with the top of the strip. The bottom edge of the strip will be even with a line on the tool. Cut.

2. Rotate the tool and align until the diagonal edge is even with the cut edge. The blunt point will be even with the bottom edge of the strip. A line on the ruler will be even with the top edge of the strip. Cut.

3. Continue in this manner for the desired number of triangles.

Easy Angle™ for half-square triangles. The seam allowance is included so you can cut triangles from the same size strips that you use for cutting squares.

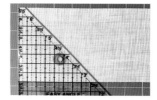
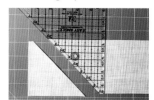

Companion Angle™ for quarter-square triangles and "flying geese" units.

Creative Grids® 60° Triangle (8" size) for cutting 60° triangles. The seam allowance is included so you can cut triangles from the same size strips that you use for cutting squares.

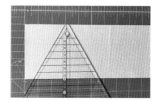
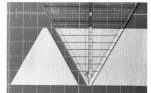

Seam Allowance

Seams are sewn with the right sides of the fabric together. Use an accurate ¼" seam allowance. Take a few minutes to test your seam allowance before you begin. Your pieces will fit together easily and you'll enjoy sewing more with an accurate ¼" seam.

To test, cut three strips 1½" × 3½". Stitch them together along the long edges. Press. The resulting square should measure exactly 3½" × 3½".

If your square is not quite 3½", your seam allowances are too fat! Test again using a slightly smaller seam allowance.

If your square is more than 3½", your seam allowances are too skinny! Test again using a slightly wider seam allowance.

Pressing

Press in the direction shown by the arrows. When there are no arrows, you may press in either direction.

To steam or not to steam . . .

Some quilters use a dry iron because they feel that steam will stretch the fabric, but I like steam because it makes a nice crease with just one touch of the iron. Without steam, I find myself pushing and rubbing with the iron to flatten the fabric, which ends up distorting the fabric.

Pinning

My favorite method of pinning is to skip it! However, for those times when you can't avoid it, be sure to use fine silk pins for the most accurate results.

Before pinning, check to be sure that all of your points are ¼" from the edge of the block. Poke a pin into the fabric ¼" from the edge (right where you'll be stitching) through the points on both layers. Leave it sticking straight up, and insert two "helper" pins—one on each side of the "poker" pin. Remember: If you tilt the "poker," your points will move and won't match! Remove the "poker" pin before sewing.

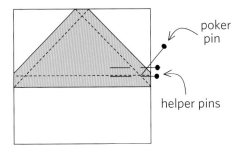

poker pin

helper pins

Folded Corners

Mark: On the wrong side of a small square, mark a diagonal line from corner to corner with a crease or light pencil mark.

Mark.

Stitch: Place the small square on top of the rectangle, right sides together. Stitch on the marked line. When chain-piecing, stop with the needle down between pieces, so that you can start sewing with the next corner right up against the needle. Lift the presser foot between pieces, so they don't get pushed out of alignment.

Stitch.

Press & Trim: Fold the corner up and press. From the wrong side, trim the layers in the corner even with the edges of the rectangle. (If you sewed exactly on the line there won't be anything to trim, but who is perfect every time?) To reduce bulk, trim the underneath layers to ¼".

Press.

To avoid marking the squares, just mark your machine! Put the needle down and slide a ruler up against the needle. Lower the presser foot to hold the ruler in place, and draw a line with a permanent marker straight out from the needle. When sewing a folded corner, opposite corners will line up with the needle and the line! As you stitch, watch the corner travel up the line instead of watching the needle.

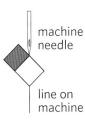

machine needle

line on machine

Backing

Cut the backing yardage in half or in thirds and remove the selvages on the edges that will be sewn together.

Batting

Purchase batting that is 8" longer and 8" wider than your quilt.

Quilting

You may quilt by hand or machine. Because there is not room to give detailed quilting information here, refer to a machine- or hand-quilting book or take a quilting class at your local quilt shop.

Follow Your Heart Sampler Quilt

Even if you don't wish to travel farther than your sewing room, you'll love piecing together this block-by-block beauty.

YARDAGE

Assorted Prints

14 fat quarters (18" × 21") **or** 28 fat eighths (9" × 21")
For more variety, scraps may be used.
Remember to include a variety of colors and values.
Be sure to include darks, brights, lights, etc.

Assorted Whites

10 half-yard cuts (18" × 42") **or** 20 fat quarters (18" × 21")
The assorted whites are shown as plain white in the diagrams. You may mix them up any way that works for you. When you need to cut matching pieces from one or two whites it will tell you; otherwise you can make it as scrappy as you wish.

Fusible Web

¾ yard 12" wide

Border Strips

These scrappy white strips are added to one or more side of each block and to the edges of the whole quilt. Cut the border strips from the assorted whites.

Add interest to your background by using several whites in each border. An easy way to make a scrappy border is to cut two strips 21" long and stitch them together end to end. Place this next to your block with the seam off center and trim the ends to the length needed. Use the leftovers for another block.

Dark Print, Light Print, Bright Print

These are cut from your assorted prints. They are given names to help you choose contrasting prints.

Batting

71" × 82"

Crosstown

Sometimes the local name for a road can't be found on the map. In Minneapolis, the "Crosstown" (Highway 62) cuts across the middle of town. In Madison, Wisconsin, Highway 12 is called the "Beltline." The "Dan Ryan Expressway" is another name for I-94 in Chicago. Getting to know a city well enough to use the local names makes it feel a little more like home.

✳ **9½" × 9½" BLOCK** ✳

CUTTING

Dark Print

2—4½" × 4½" squares
2—1½" × 9½" strips

Light Print

2—1½" × 9½" strips
4—1½" × 3½" strips

Assorted Whites

4—3½" × 3½" squares

SEWING

A. Stitch a dark print 1½" × 9½" strip between two light print 1½" × 9½" strips as shown. Press seams toward the dark print. Strip set measures 3½" × 9½".
Cut 2—4½" units.

B. Stitch a light print 1½" × 3½" strip to each white 3½" square. Press seam toward the light print. Units measure 3½" × 4½". Make 4.

C. Stitch the Step A and B units together to make two rows exactly as shown. Press seams toward the center. Rows measure 4½" × 9½".

D. Stitch the remaining dark 1½" × 9½" strip between the two rows as shown. Press seams toward the dark strip. The block measures 9½" × 9½".

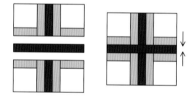

E. Cut the two dark 4½" squares in half diagonally to make 4 triangles.

Matching centers, stitch one triangle to each side of the block as shown. Press seams toward the triangles.

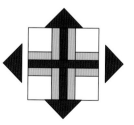

F. Rotate the block as shown and trim to 10" × 10".

10" × 10"

BORDER STRIPS

G. Stitch assorted white pieces together as desired for the length of the border strips in Step H.

H. Stitch a white 3" × 10" strip to the left edge. Stitch a white 2" × 12½" strip to the bottom edge. Stitch a white 3½" × 11½" strip to the right edge. Press seams toward the white strips. Block measures 15½" wide × 11½" tall.

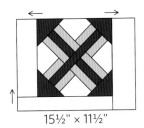

15½" × 11½"

Red Arrow Highway

When I was growing up, we could ride our bikes to Lake Michigan and spend the afternoon at the beach. The two-lane Red Arrow Highway in the southwest corner of Michigan is the grown-up version of those happy days. It's fun to drive along the lake and explore harbor towns with art, antiques, and wineries. Parks with hiking, sand dunes, and beautiful views of the lake take me back in time.

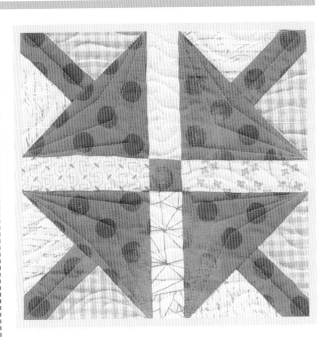

✷ 9" × 9" BLOCK ✷

CUTTING

Print
2—5¼" × 5¼" squares
2—1½" × 8" strips
1—1½" × 1½" square

Assorted Whites
2—5¼" × 5¼" squares
4—1½" × 4½" strips

SEWING

A. Cut the two white 5¼" squares in half diagonally. Matching centers, stitch the print 1½" × 8" strips between the resulting triangles. Press seams toward the print strip. Make 2.

Make 2.

B. Center a print 5¼" square on top of each Step A unit with right sides together. Mark a diagonal line exactly as shown. Stitch a scant ¼" on each side of the line. Cut on the line. Yield: 4 units.

 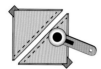

Make 2.

C. Press seams toward the print. See Terry's Tip at right. Trim the resulting squares to 4½" × 4½". Make 4.

Make 4.

4½" × 4½"

D. Arrange the Step C squares and white 1½" × 4½" strips around a print 1½" square as shown. Stitch into rows. Press seams toward the white strips.

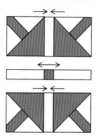

✳ TERRY'S TIP
Precision Pressing

When pressing, move the iron parallel to the edge of the square. This will keep the fabric from stretching out of shape.

E. Stitch the rows together. Press seams toward the center. Block measures 9½" × 9½".

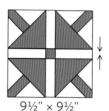

9½" × 9½"

BORDER STRIPS

This block has no borders.

London Roads

Our daughter Meg spent a semester studying abroad in London. She loved exploring the city on the "Tube" and soaking in the sights from the top deck of a bright red double-decker bus. On her last night in London, she said goodbye to her favorite city from the top of the London Eye.

✳ 12" × 12" BLOCK ✳

CUTTING

4 Dark Prints

From *each* print, cut 1—2½" × 10½" strip; from *each* strip, cut:

    1—2" × 4½" rectangle
    1 triangle using the Companion Angle Ruler

Bright Print

8—1¾" × 4½" rectangles
1—2½" × 21" strip; from this strip, cut:
    4 triangles using the Companion Angle Ruler

Assorted Whites

5—4½" × 4½" squares; from 4 of these squares, cut:
    4 triangles using the Easy Angle Ruler
(If you are only using one white print, cut 1—4½" × 21" strip; from this strip, cut: 1—4½" × 4½" square and cut 4 triangles using the Easy Angle Ruler.)

SEWING

A. Position a bright print triangle on top of each dark print triangle with edges even and right sides together.

 Layer.

Stitch a scant ¼" seam as shown. See Terry's Tip above right.

 Stitch.

Press seams toward the dark print. *These must all face the same way!*

 Press.

Stitch a white triangle to each. Press seam toward the white. Units measure 4½" × 4½". Make 4.

 Make 4.

B. Stitch each dark print 2" × 4½" rectangle between two bright print 1¾" × 4½" rectangles as shown. Press seams toward the dark print. Units measure 4½" × 4½". Make 4.

 Make 4.

✳ TERRY'S TIP
The Home Stretch

Use a scant ¼" seam allowance when stitching the bias seams in Step A. The bias edge will stretch a little while sewing. Afterward, the seam will relax and be slightly wider. Press following the grain of the fabric to avoid distorting the shape.

C. Arrange the Step A and Step B units around the remaining white 4½" square as shown. Stitch into rows. Press seams in alternate directions.

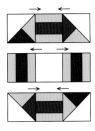

D. Stitch the rows together and press seams toward the center. Block measures 12½" × 12½".

BORDER STRIP

E. Stitch white strips together as desired for the length of the border piece in Step F.

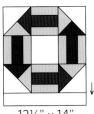

12½" × 14"

F. Stitch a white 2" × 12½" strip to the bottom edge. Press seam toward the white strip. Block measures 12½" wide × 14" tall.

Springfield

While wandering through antique malls, I love to look at old magazines and advertising posters. In Springfield, Missouri, I came across a colorful wooden sign that caught my eye. Immediately inspiration struck, and I wanted to make those shapes out of fabric.

✳ 7" × 17½" BLOCK ✳

CUTTING

5 Prints
From *each* print, cut:
1—4½" × 4½" square

5 Whites
From *each* white, cut:
1—4½" × 4½" square
2—1½" × 1½" squares

SEWING

A. Mark a diagonal line on the wrong side of a white 4½" square. Position the marked white square on top of a print square with right sides together and edges even.

B. Stitch a scant ¼" on each side of the line. Cut on the line.

C. Press one seam toward the print and one seam toward the white.

Trim the squares to 4" × 4".

4" × 4"

D. Mark a diagonal line on the wrong side of two matching white 1½" squares. Position one on each print corner with right sides together. Stitch on the line.

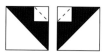

Trim seams to ¼" and press in the same direction as the previous seam.

Repeat Steps A–D with each print square.
Yield: 10 (2 squares from each print).

E. Stitch matching squares together into pairs. Press seams in opposite directions as shown. Make 5. Units measure 4" × 7½".

F. Stitch units into a long row. Press seams in the direction that looks best. Row measures 7½" × 18".

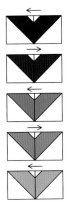

BORDER STRIPS

G. Stitch assorted white pieces together as desired for the length of the border strips in Step H.

H. Stitch a white 2" × 18" strip to the right edge. Stitch a white 3" × 9" strip to the bottom edge. Press seams toward the white strips. Trim the block to 8½" × 20".

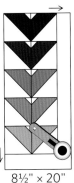

8½" × 20"

Spaghetti Junction

When viewed from above, the crisscross of highways near our capitol in St. Paul, Minnesota, looks like a tangled plate of spaghetti. But spaghetti is best left in the kitchen. The downtown St. Paul version is often a white-knuckle drive. I'm glad we've only had to navigate it once with our camper!

✳ **13" × 12½" BLOCK** ✳

CUTTING

2 Prints

From *each* print, cut:
1—1½" × 21" strip
1—1½" × 4¾" strip
1—3¾" × 5" strip; from this strip, cut:
    1 triangle using the 60° triangle ruler

2 Whites

From *each* white, cut:
1—2" × 21" strip
2—2¾" × 3¾" rectangles
2—2" × 4¾" strips
3—2" × 3" rectangles

SEWING

A. Stitch each print 1½" × 4¾" strip between two white 2" × 4¾" strips. Press toward the print. Units measure 4½" × 4¾".

B. Layer two matching white 2¾" × 3¾" rectangles, **wrong sides together** on the cutting mat. Align the diagonal edge of the 60° triangle ruler with the upper left corner as shown. The bottom edge of the ruler should be even with the bottom edge of the rectangles. Trim. **Discard the small triangle.** Repeat with the second pair of 2¾" × 3¾" white rectangles. See Terry's Tip below.

Discard.

C. Stitch the Step B units to the print 60° triangles as shown. Press seams toward the white. Trim units to 4½" × 3¾".

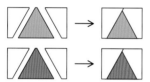

✳ **TERRY'S TIP**

Way to Rule!

We're using the ruler to trim the correct angle—no need to measure anything. Discard the **smaller** triangles. The remaining triangles will have a blunt point at the bottom, making them just the right size!

✳ **TERRY'S TIP**

Which Way Is Up?

Position the print triangle with the blunt end at the top. Position the white triangles with the blunt end at the bottom.

FIRST SIDE (shown): With right sides together, two edges of the white are even with both sides of the print triangle. Bottom edges intersect at the ¼" stitching line. Begin stitching at the top.

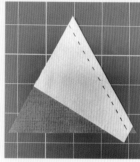

SECOND SIDE: Align the white points at the top. Bottom edges intersect at the ¼" stitching line. Begin stitching at the top.

D. Stitch the Step A and Step C units together as shown. Press seams away from the triangles. Arrow units measure 4½" × 8".

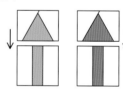

E. Stitch the arrows together exactly as shown. Press in the direction that looks best. The unit measures 8½" wide × 8" tall.

F. Stitch each print 1½" × 21" strip to a white 2" × 21" strip. Press toward the print. Strip sets measure 3" × 21".

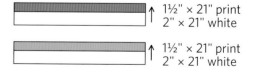

1½" × 21" print
2" × 21" white

1½" × 21" print
2" × 21" white

G. Cut a 10" unit and a 7" unit from each strip set.

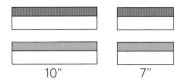

10"   7"

H. Stitch a white 2" × 3" rectangle to one end of each 7" Step G unit exactly as shown. **Pay attention! It's easy to sew these backwards.** Press toward the white rectangle. Stitch these units to the arrows. Press away from center. Unit measures 8½" × 13".

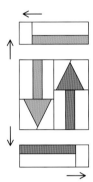

I. Stitch a white 2" × 3" rectangle to both ends of each 10" Step G unit. Press away from center. Stitch these units to the side edges of the block. Press away from center. Block measures 13½" wide × 13" tall.

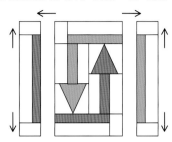

BORDER STRIPS

J. Stitch assorted white pieces together as desired for the length of the border strips in Step K.

K. Stitch 2¼" × 13½" strips to the top and bottom edges. Stitch 2½" × 16½" strips to the side edges. Press seams toward white strips. Trim the block to 16½" wide × 15½" tall.

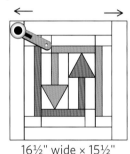

16½" wide × 15½"

Tennessee Two-Tone

"Tennessee Two-Tone" is a nod to both the colors in our arrow and to all of the music we've enjoyed in Tennessee. You might instantly think of Nashville, but Kirk's favorite is the Big Ears Festival in Knoxville, Tennessee.

✳ **6" × 32" BLOCK** ✳

CUTTING

2 Prints

From *each* print, cut:
1—1½" × 20½" strip
1—3½" × 21" strip; from each strip, cut:
    2—3½" × 3½" squares
    6 triangles using the Easy Angle Ruler

Assorted Whites

2—2½" × 10½" strips
2—2½" × 6½" strips
2—2½" × 4½" strips
1—3½" × 11" strip; from this strip, cut:
    4 triangles using the Easy Angle Ruler

SEWING

A. Stitch the white 2½" × 10½", 2½" × 6½", and 2½" × 4½" strips together to make two rows as shown. Press all seams in the same direction. Rows should measure 2½" × 20½".

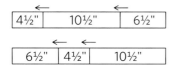

B. Stitch a print 1½" × 20½" strip to a Step A row. Press seams toward the print. Make one with each print. Rows measure 3½" × 20½". **Do not sew the two prints together yet!**

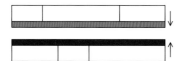

C. Mark a diagonal line on the wrong side of each print 3½" square. Position a square of the opposite color at each end of both rows. Lines must be positioned **exactly as shown.** Stitch on the line.

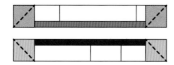

Press toward the corner. Make sure the triangles are facing **exactly as shown.** Trim seam to ¼".

D. Stitch the print and white triangles together to make squares exactly as shown. Press in the direction shown by the arrows. Squares measure 3½" × 3½".

Make 4.   Make 2.   Make 2.

E. Stitch the Step D squares at the ends of each row **exactly as shown.** Press seams open. Stitch the rows together. Press seam open or in the direction that looks best. Block should measure 6½" × 32½".

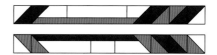

BORDER STRIPS

F. Stitch assorted white pieces together as desired for the length of the border strips in Step G.

G. Stitch 3½" × 32½" strips to the top and bottom. Stitch a 3½" × 12½" strip to the right side. Press seams toward the white strips. Trim the block to 35" wide × 12½" tall.

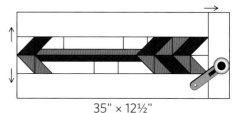

35" × 12½"

Circle Pines

We've camped among the pines in northern Wisconsin, driven through the pines to the top of Mount Lemmon near Tucson, and hiked through the pine forest near Colorado Springs. There's nothing more humbling than being deep in the woods, looking up, and seeing a circle of pines towering above.

CUTTING

4 Prints

From *each* print, cut:
1—3½" × 6½" rectangle
1—2½" × 4½" rectangle
1—1½" × 2½" rectangle

Assorted Whites

8—3½" × 3½" squares
8—2½" × 3½" rectangles
8—1½" × 3½" rectangles

SEWING

A. Mark a diagonal line on the wrong side of the white 3½" squares. Position a marked square on each print 3½" × 6½" rectangle as shown. Stitch on the line. Press toward the corner. Trim seam allowance to ¼". Make 4.

   Make 4.

✳ **12" × 12" BLOCK** ✳

Repeat at the opposite end using the remaining white 3½" squares. The point should be ¼" in from the edge. Units measure 3½" × 6½".

 Point is ¼" from edge.

✳ **TERRY'S TIP**

Travel Light

For a calmer look, use only four white or light prints instead of an assorted mix. To do this, from *each* of four whites, cut:

2—3½" × 3½" squares
2—2½" × 3½" rectangles
2—1½" × 3½" rectangles

Use pieces from one white print and one medium or dark print to make each tree unit.

B. Position a white 2½" × 3½" rectangle on each print 2½" × 4½" rectangle exactly as shown. Mark a dot on the white rectangle 2½" down from the corner exactly as shown. Stitch from the corner to the dot as shown. Press toward the white. Trim seam allowance to ¼". Make 4.

  Make 4.

Repeat at the opposite end of the print rectangle exactly as shown. The edges should be straight. Unit measures 2½" × 6½". Make 4.

  Make 4.

C. Repeat Step B using the print 1½" × 2½" rectangle and white 1½" × 3½" rectangles. Mark your dots 1½" down from the corner. Unit measures 1½" × 6½". Make 4.

Make 4.

D. Stitch the Step A, B, and C units together as shown to make four tree units. Press seams in the direction that looks best. Units measure 6½" × 6½".

Make 4.

E. Stitch the tree units together in pairs. Press seams in opposite directions. Stitch the pairs together. Press in the direction that looks best. Block measures 12½" × 12½".

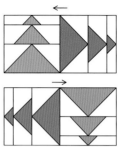

BORDER STRIPS

F. Stitch assorted white pieces together as desired for the length of the border strips in Step G.

G. Stitch 2½" × 12½" strips to the top and bottom edges. Press seams toward the white strips. Trim the block to 12½" wide × 15½" tall.

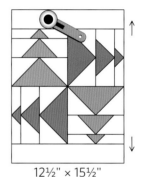
12½" × 15½"

Hampton Roads

Hampton Roads is a cluster of seven cities in Virginia and North Carolina. Each of them is represented by a circle on our arrow. And together, what a place! There's such a variety: Civil War history, plantations, the oceanfront and boardwalk, a wonderful mix of past and present.

✳ **8" × 27" BLOCK** ✳

CUTTING

Dark Print

1—4½" × 19½" strip
1—4½" × 21" strip; from this strip, cut:
    2 triangles using the Easy Angle Ruler
    1 triangle using the Companion Angle Ruler
4—2½" × 2½" squares

Assorted Bright Prints

7—2½" × 2½" squares

Fusible Web

¼ yard

Assorted Whites

2—2½" × 9½" strips
2—2½" × 6½" strips
2—2½" × 4½" strips
1—4½" × 21" strip; from this strip, cut:
    2 triangles using the Easy Angle Ruler
    1 triangle using the Companion Angle Ruler

SEWING

A. Stitch the white 2½" × 9½", 2½" × 6½", and 2½" × 4½" strips together as shown to make two rows. Press all seams in the same direction. Rows measure 2½" × 19½".

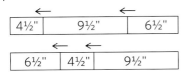

B. Mark a diagonal line on the wrong side of each dark print 2½" square.

Mark.

C. Position a marked square at the end of each white row **exactly as shown.** Stitch on the line. Trim seam to ¼" and press toward the corner.

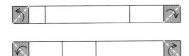

D. Stitch the dark print 4½" × 19½" strip between the Step C white rows. Press seams toward the center. Unit measures 8½" × 19½".

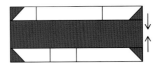

E. Stitch the dark print triangles and white triangles together as shown. Press seams away from the center. Units measure 4½" × 8½".

F. Stitch the units together as shown. Press seams in the direction that looks best. The block should measure 8½" × 27½".

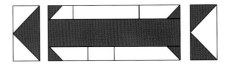

G. Trace seven 2" circles ½" apart onto the paper side of fusible web. Cut out a scant ¼" outside the line.

Trace.   Cut.

H. Fuse the circle shapes to the wrong side of the bright print 2½" squares. Cut out on the line. Peel the paper off.

Fuse.   Cut out.

✱ TERRY'S TIP
Testing, Testing

Fuse the discarded sections to a scrap to test stitching. For a zigzag stitch, set the width at about 1.5 mm and length at about 1 mm. For a buttonhole stitch, set the width and length at about 2 mm. A piece of stabilizer or tracing paper underneath while stitching will help keep the fabric flat.

I. Position a circle in the exact center of the arrow. Space the other circles ½" apart. Fuse in place.

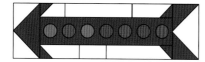

J. Stitch around the circles using a zigzag or buttonhole stitch.

BORDER STRIPS

K. Stitch assorted white pieces together as desired for the length of the border strips in Step L.

L. Stitch a 2" × 8½" strip to the right edge. Stitch a 2½" × 29" strip to the bottom edge. Press seams toward the white strips. Trim the block to 28½" wide × 10" tall.

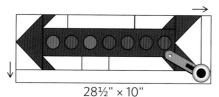

28½" × 10"

Circle:

HAMPTON ROADS
2" Circle template
Trace seven circles.

San Francisco

After driving around the same block four times looking for the Cheesecake Factory in San Francisco, my daughter Meg and I decided to park and walk. We finally found it upstairs in Macy's. No wonder we couldn't see it from the street! We were seated next to the famous San Francisco twins, Marian and Vivian Brown, who were dressed to the nines in matching suits and hats with bright red lipstick and big friendly smiles. This trip will always hold a place in my heart.

✳ **10½" × 10½" BLOCK** ✳

CUTTING

Bright Print

3—2" × 12" strips
2—2" × 5" strips

Dark Print

2—2" × 12" strips
1—2" × 5" strip

White

1—5" × 5" square
1—3½" × 7" strip
3—2" × 5" strips

SEWING

A. Stitch a strip set as shown using three bright print 2" × 12" strips and two dark print 2" × 12" strips. Press seams toward the bright print. The strip set should measure 8" × 12".

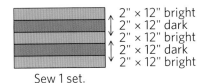

2" × 12" bright
2" × 12" dark
2" × 12" bright
2" × 12" dark
2" × 12" bright

Sew 1 set.

Cut the strip set into a 5" set and a 7" set.

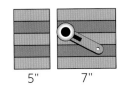

5"   7"

B. Stitch white 2" × 5" strips to the top and bottom of the 5" Step A set. Press seams toward the bright print. The strip set measures 11" × 5". Cut two 2" units.

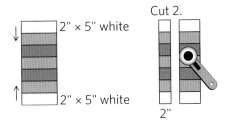

Cut 2.

2" × 5" white

2" × 5" white

2"

C. Stitch the white 3½" × 7" strip to the 7" Step A set as shown. Press seam toward the bright print. The strip set now measures 11" × 7". Cut three 2" units.

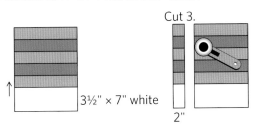

Cut 3.

3½" × 7" white

2"

D. Stitch a strip set as shown using one white 2" × 5" strip, one white 5" square, one dark 2" × 5" strip, and two bright 2" × 5" strips. Press all seams toward the bright print. Strip set measures 11" × 5". Cut into two 2" units.

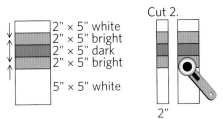

Cut 2.

2" × 5" white
2" × 5" bright
2" × 5" dark
2" × 5" bright

5" × 5" white

2"

E. Stitch the Step B, C, and D units together as shown to make a heart. Press all seams in the same direction. Block measures 11" × 11".

D C B C B C D

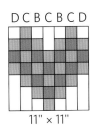

11" × 11"

BORDER STRIPS

F. Stitch assorted white pieces together as desired for the length of the border strips in Step G.

G. Stitch a 3" × 11" strip to the right edge. Stitch a 3½" × 13½" strip to the bottom edge. Press seams toward the white strips. Trim the block to 12½" wide × 13" tall.

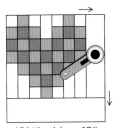

12½" wide × 13"

Santa Fe

I love the colors of the Southwest: turquoise (of course), warm reds, terra-cotta, orange, and ocher. These colors are in abundance in Santa Fe. Is it the sunny sky that makes the colors so vibrant, or is it the warm light reflecting off of the adobe buildings? Either way, I can't wait to go back.

✳ **15" × 15" BLOCK** ✳

CUTTING

Assorted Bright Prints

3—3½" × 14" strips
1—3½" × 7" rectangle

Dark Print

13—1½" × 1½" squares

Assorted Whites

4—4½" × 4½" squares
1—4½" × 7" rectangle
1—3½" × 14" strip
1—2½" × 14" strip
1—1½" × 14" strip

SEWING

A. Stitch a white 1½" × 14" strip to a print 3½" × 14" strip. **This print will be next to the corner white squares.** Press seam toward the print. Strip set measures 4½" × 14". Cut into eight 1½" units.

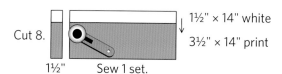

Cut 8.   Sew 1 set.

1½"   ↓ 1½" × 14" white

3½" × 14" print

B. Stitch a Step A unit to each white 4½" square as shown. Press seam toward the print. Make 4.

Stitch a dark print 1½" square to the four remaining Step A units. Press toward the print strip.

Stitch the units together exactly as shown. Press toward the print strip at bottom. Squares should now measure 5½" × 5½". Make 4.

Make 4.

C. Stitch a white 2½" × 14" strip to a print 3½" × 14" strip. Press seam toward the print. Strip set measures 5½" × 14". Cut into eight 1½" units.

Cut 8.

2½" × 14" white

3½" × 14" print

1½"   Sew 1 set.

D. Stitch a Step C unit to each square as shown. Press seam toward the new print. Make 4.

Stitch a dark print 1½" square to the remaining four Step C units. Press toward the print strips.

Stitch these units to the square exactly as shown. Press seam toward the new print. Squares should now measure 6½" × 6½". Make 4.

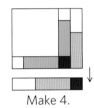

Make 4.

E. Stitch a white 3½" × 14" strip to a print 3½" × 14" strip. Press seam toward the print. Strip set measures 6½" × 14". Cut into eight 1½" units.

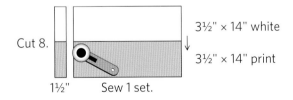

Cut 8.

3½" × 14" white

3½" × 14" print

1½"   Sew 1 set.

F. Stitch a Step E unit to each square as shown. Press seam toward the new print. Make 4.

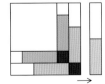

Stitch a dark print 1½" square to the remaining four Step E units. Press toward the print strip.

Stitch these units to the square exactly as shown. Press seam toward the new print. Units measure 7½" × 7½". Make 4.

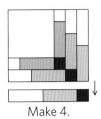

Make 4.

G. Stitch a white 4½" × 7" rectangle to a print 3½" × 7" rectangle as shown. Press seam toward the print. Strip set measures 7½" × 7". Cut four 1½" units.

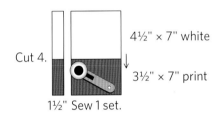

Cut 4.

4½" × 7" white

3½" × 7" print

1½" Sew 1 set.

H. Arrange the Step F squares and Step G units around a dark print 1½" square as shown.

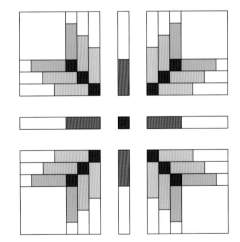

I. Stitch into rows. Press seams in opposite directions.

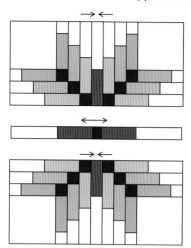

J. Stitch the rows together. Press seams toward center. The block measures 15½" × 15½".

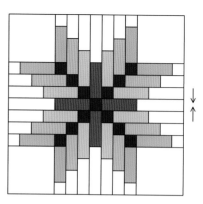

BORDER STRIPS

This block has no borders.

Silicon Hills

One of the nicknames for Austin, Texas, is "Silicon Hills" because it's become a magnet for start-ups and tech companies. It has the famous motto "Keep Austin Weird," and claims to be the live music capital of the world. This collision of art and science with the mixture of old and new make Austin a vibrant and energetic place. But I love Austin because of the walkable neighborhoods, the interesting people, and of course, the food trucks. Who could resist the "Hey Cupcake!" AirStream on South Congress Avenue?

✳ **10" × 15" BLOCK** ✳

CUTTING

Assorted Darks
6—5" × 5" squares

Assorted Brights
6—4" × 4" squares

Assorted Whites
6—5½" × 5½" squares

Fusible Web
½ yard

SEWING

A. Trace 6 large circles onto the paper side of the fusible web, leaving ½" between them. Use template on page 28. Cut out about ¼" outside the marked line.

 Trace. Cut.

B. Fuse the circle shapes onto the wrong side of the dark print 5" squares, following the manufacturer's instructions. Cut out on the marked lines. Make 6.

 Fuse. Cut out.

C. Peel the paper off and center each print circle on a white 5½" square. Fuse in place. Make 6.

D. Prepare the contrast arrow shapes in the same manner using bright print 4" squares and the templates on page 28. Peel the paper off and center each arrow on a Step C unit. Fuse in place. Make 6.

E. Stitch along the edges of the arrows and circles using a zigzag or buttonhole stitch. Use matching thread.

F. Stitch the squares together into two rows of three as shown. Press seams in opposite directions. Stitch the rows together and press. The block measures 10½" × 15½".

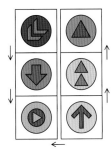

BORDER STRIPS

G. Stitch assorted white pieces together as desired for the length of the border strips in Step H.

H. Stitch a 3½" × 15½" strip to each side edge. Stitch a 4" × 16½" strip to the bottom edge. Press seams toward the white strips. Trim the block to 15½" wide × 18½" tall.

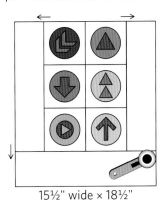

15½" wide × 18½"

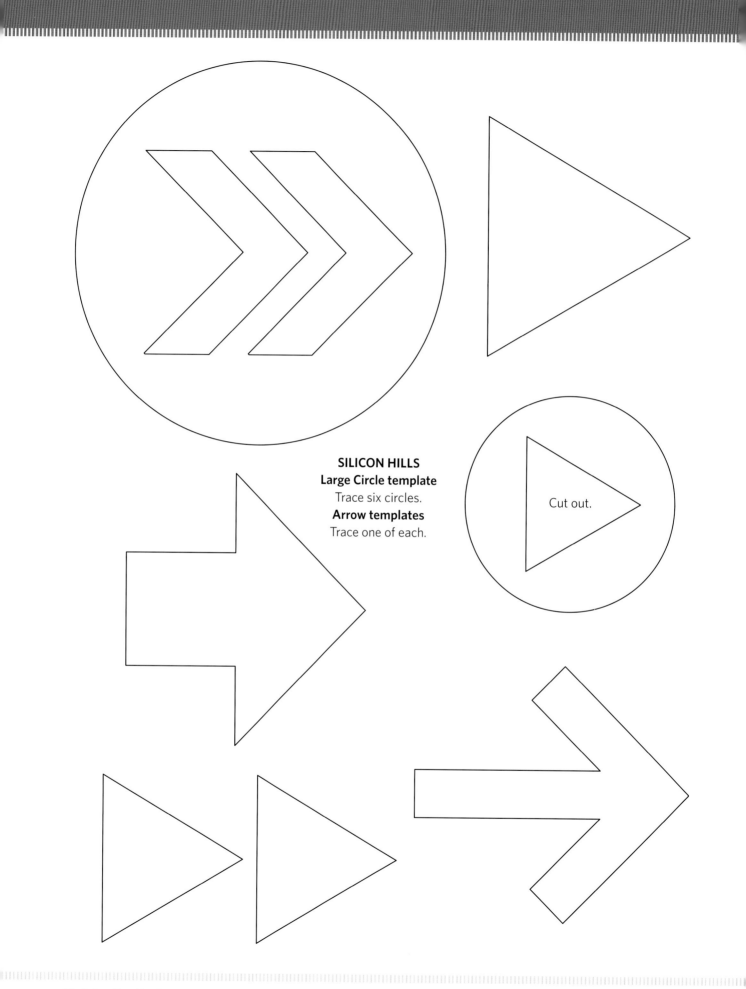

SILICON HILLS
Large Circle template
Trace six circles.
Arrow templates
Trace one of each.

Cut out.

I Heart New York

There are so many things we love about New York City. Penguins in Central Park, Rent on Broadway, the Red and White Quilt Show, MoMA, Junior's Cheesecake at Grand Central Terminal, the view from the Empire State Building, and Times Square at night . . . the list is endless!

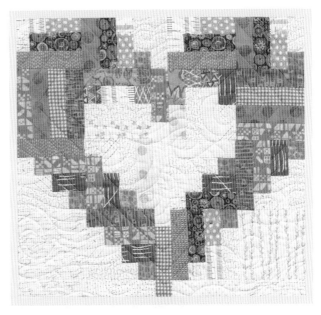

✴ **17" × 16" BLOCK** ✴

CUTTING

Assorted Prints

2—3½" × 10" strips
2—2½" × 10" strips
2—1½" × 10" strips
6—1½" × 21" strips; from these strips, cut:
    20—1½" × 4½" strips
    1—1½" × 3½" rectangle
    2—1½" × 1½" squares

Assorted Whites

2—3½" × 10" strips
2—2½" × 10" strips
2—1½" × 10" strips
2—4½" × 4½" squares
8—1½" × 4½" strips
3—1½" × 3½" rectangles
1—1½" × 2½" rectangle

SEWING

A. Stitch assorted print 1½" × 4½" strips together as shown to make 2 units. Press all seams in the same direction. Units measure 4½" × 4½".

Make 2.

B. Stitch strip sets using the white 10" and assorted print 10" strips as shown below. All strip sets measure 4½" × 10". Cut into 1½" units.

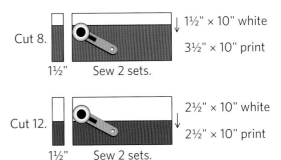

Cut 8.
1½"
Sew 2 sets.
1½" × 10" white
3½" × 10" print

Cut 12.
1½"
Sew 2 sets.
2½" × 10" white
2½" × 10" print

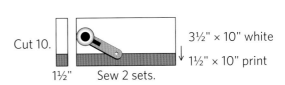

Cut 10.
1½"
Sew 2 sets.
3½" × 10" white
1½" × 10" print

✴ **TERRY'S TIP**
Stay on Track

Test your ¼" seam allowance before you begin. Stitch three 1½" × 3½" scraps together along the long edges. The resulting square must measure exactly 3½" × 3½".

In the following steps, stitch Step B units, white 1½" × 4½" strips, and assorted print 1½" × 4½" strips together **exactly as shown.** Pay attention! It's easy to sew these backwards. Press all seams the same way.

C. Stitch a print 1½" × 4½" strip to Step B units. Units will measure 3½" × 4½". Make 2.

Make 2.

D. Stitch print 1½" × 4½" strips to Step B units. Units will measure 4½" × 4½". Make 2.

Make 2.

E. Stitch a white 1½" × 4½" strip to Step B units. Units will measure 4½" × 4½". Make 2.

Make 2.

F. Stitch a print 1½" × 4½" strip to Step B units. Units will measure 4½" × 4½". Make 4.

Make 4.

G. Stitch Step B units together as shown. Unit will measure 4½" × 4½". Make 1.

Make 1.

H. Stitch a white 1½" × 2½" rectangle between two print 1½" squares. Stitch one print and two white 1½" × 4½" strips to the sides. Make 1. Unit measures 4½" × 4½".

Make 1.

I. Arrange the Step A–H units as shown below. Trim the Step D units to 3½" tall. Place white 4½" squares in the lower corners, and a white 1½" × 4½" strip at the bottom of each row.

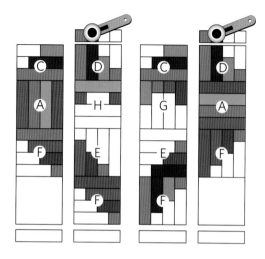

J. Arrange white and print rectangles exactly as shown to make the center row. Stitch the units into rows. Press the seams in opposite directions as shown.

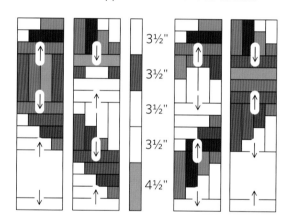

K. Stitch the rows together. Press in the direction that looks best. Block measures 17½" wide × 16½" tall.

BORDER STRIPS

L. Stitch assorted white pieces together as desired for the length of the border strips in Step M.

M. Stitch a 4½" × 17½" strip to the bottom edge. Stitch a 4" × 20½" strip to the right edge. Press seams toward the white strips. Trim the block to 20½" wide × 20" tall.

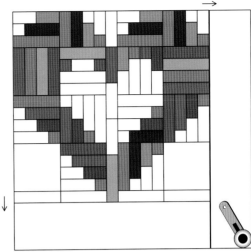

20½" wide × 20" tall

Snowbirds

That's us! My husband, Kirk, and I traveled south for the first time this past winter. I love the four seasons and missed showshoeing (and even shoveling!). Kirk was thrilled to be away from the cold weather. This coming winter we will set off again, this time with a completely new route!

CUTTING

4 Bright Prints

From *each* print, cut:
1—4½" × 21" strip; from each of these strips, cut:
    1—4½" × 4½" square
Trim each remaining strip to 3" wide and cut:
    4 triangles using the Easy Angle Ruler
Trim each remaining strip to 1¾" wide and cut:
    2 triangles using the Companion Angle Ruler

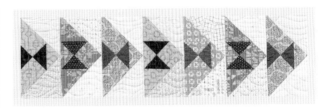

✳ **3¾" × 7½" TRIANGLE BLOCKS** ✳

Dark Print
4—4½" × 4½" squares

Assorted Whites
8—5" × 5" squares

SEWING

A. Mark a diagonal line on the wrong side of each bright print 4½" square. Position each marked square on a dark print 4½" square, with right sides together and edges even.

Stitch a scant ¼" on each side of the line. Cut on the line.

Press seams toward the dark. Yield: 2 squares from each bright print.

B. Layer matching Step A squares as shown, with edges even. The print and dark must be in opposite positions as shown. Mark a diagonal line.

Stitch a scant ¼" on each side of the line. Cut on the line.

Press. Trim squares to 3" × 3". Yield: 2 squares from each print.

C. Stitch matching bright print 3" triangles to opposite sides of the Step B squares exactly as shown. Press seams away from the center. Make 8.

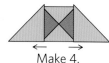
Make 4.

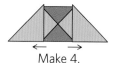
Make 4.

✷ TERRY'S TIP
Twists & Turns

Stitch print triangles to the **dark** edges of four squares, and to the **print** edges of four squares.

D. Stitch a matching print 1¾" triangle to the top of each unit. Press seams toward triangles. Make 8.

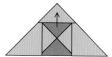

E. Cut the white 5" × 5" squares in half diagonally.

Stitch the resulting triangles to the Step D units as shown. Press seams toward the white triangles. Trim blocks to 4¼" × 8".

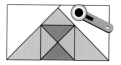

F. Stitch 7 blocks together in a row as shown. Press seams in the direction that looks best. Set aside the extra one for a quilt label. Row measures 26¾" × 8".

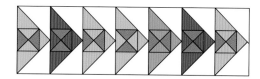

BORDER STRIPS

G. Stitch assorted white pieces together as desired for the length of the border strips in Step H.

H. Stitch a 2½" × 26¾" strip to the top edge. Stitch a 4½" × 10" strip to each side edge. Press seams toward the white strips. Trim the row to 34½" wide × 9½" tall.

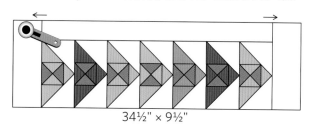
34½" × 9½"

Maui

On a gray and foggy day we drove to the top of the Haleakala Crater in Maui. We drove higher and higher until we were up above the clouds. At the top, the sun was shining and it was really cold. Only on Maui can you go from swimming in the ocean to hiking in a winter jacket on the same day.

CUTTING

Assorted Prints

6—3½" × 6" rectangles
6—1¼" × 6" strips
12—2½" × 4½" rectangles
6—2" × 10" strips

Dark Print

6—2½" × 4½" rectangles

White

12—6" × 7½" rectangles

SEWING

A. Position an assorted print 2½" × 4½" rectangle on each dark print 2½" × 4½" rectangle, with right sides together, exactly as shown. Mark a dot 2½" below the corner as shown. Stitch from the corner to the dot. Press toward the print. **The edges should be straight!** Trim seams to ¼". Make 6.

Make 6.

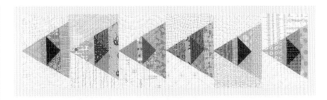

✳ **6¾" × 10½" TRIANGLE BLOCKS** ✳

B. Repeat at the opposite end of the dark rectangle exactly as shown. Begin stitching at the dot. Press toward the print. **The edges should be straight, and the point should be ¼" from the edge!** Trim seam to ¼". Unit measures 2½" × 8½". Make 6.

Make 6.

✳ **TERRY'S TIP**
Beware of Curves

When making the pieced rectangles in Steps A and B, be sure to position the rectangles so their ends are perfectly square with each other. If you don't, the finished units could end up being bowed or arched.

Correct

Incorrect

C. Matching centers, stitch a print 3½" × 6" rectangle, print 1¼" × 6" strip, Step B unit, and print 2" × 10" strip together exactly as shown. **Pay attention to the dark triangle!** It must point toward the 2" × 10" strip as shown. Press all seams away from the triangle. Repeat to make 6.

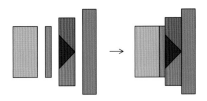

D. Position the 60° triangle ruler on top of the Step C unit. **Align the ¼" dotted line with the dark triangle points as shown.** The 7¼" line should be parallel to the bottom edge. It doesn't matter if the line is exactly on the edge because it will be trimmed in Step F. It's more important for the triangle points to be exactly ¼" from the edge. Trim. Make 6.

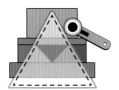 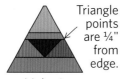

Triangle points are ¼" from edge.

Make 6.

E. Layer two white 6" × 7½" rectangles, **wrong sides together,** on the cutting mat. Align the diagonal edge of the 60° triangle ruler with the upper left corner as shown. The bottom edge of the ruler should be even with the bottom edge of the rectangles. Trim. Discard the small triangle. Repeat to make 12 trimmed units.

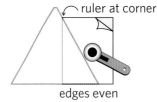

ruler at corner

Yield 12 total.

edges even   Discard.

F. Stitch a trimmed unit to each side of the Step D triangles. Press toward the white. Make 6.

Trim block to 7¼" × 11". The top point of the triangle should be ¼" from the edge. Make 6.

Make 6.

★ **TERRY'S TIP**
Start at the Top

Position the pieced Step D triangle with the blunt end at the top. Position the white units with the blunt end at the bottom.
FIRST SIDE: With right sides together, two edges of the white unit are even with both sides of the triangle (see the photo on the top of page 16). Bottom edges intersect at the ¼" stitching line. Begin stitching at the top.
SECOND SIDE: Align the white points at the top. Begin stitching at the top.

G. Stitch the Step F blocks together into a row. Press in the direction that looks best. Row measures 11" × 41".

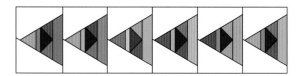

BORDER STRIPS

H. Stitch assorted white pieces together as desired for the length of the border strips in Step I.

I. Stitch a 2" × 11" strip to each end of the row. Press seams toward the white strips. Trim the row to 43½" wide × 11" tall.

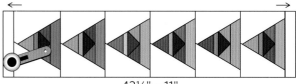

43½" × 11"

Savannah Strings

Savannah, Georgia, is one of our favorite places to visit. Its Southern charm has wowed us each time we've been there. We've enjoyed walking in the historic district and admiring all of the beautiful old homes. Every few blocks there is a peaceful little park with a fountain in the middle. When we get hungry there's no shortage of great restaurants!

CUTTING

Assorted Prints
1—1" × 9" strip
6—1" × 10" strips

White
2—2½" × 3½" rectangles
2—2" × 7½" rectangles
1—1" × 2¼" rectangle

SEWING

A. Stitch the six assorted print 1" × 10" strips together as shown. Press all seams in the same direction. Strip set measures 3½" × 10".

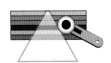
↑ 6—1" × 10"

Sew 1 set.

B. Position the 60° triangle ruler at the center of the strip set. Align the blunt tip of the ruler with the top edge and the 3½" line with the bottom edge. Cut a triangle as shown.

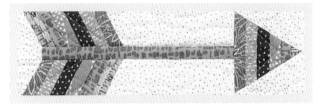

✳ **12" × 3½" BLOCK** ✳

C. Align the 2" line on your ruler with the diagonal edge of each side piece and trim. Cut 2. Discard the end pieces.

Discard.　　　Discard.

D. Layer the two white 2½" × 3½" rectangles with **wrong sides together** on the cutting mat. Align the diagonal edge of the 60° triangle ruler with the upper left corner as shown. The bottom edge of the ruler should be even with the bottom edge of the rectangles. Trim. **Discard the small triangle.**

Discard.

✳ TERRY'S TIP
Let's Be Blunt

We're using the ruler to trim the correct angle— no need to measure anything. The resulting triangles will have a blunt point at the bottom, making them just the right size! Be sure to discard the smaller triangles.

E. Stitch the white Step D units to the Step B triangle as shown. See photo below for alignment. Press seams toward the white. Trim to 4" × 3½".

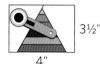

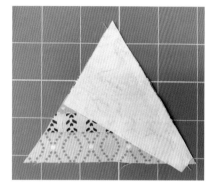

F. Layer two matching white 2" × 7½" rectangles, **wrong sides together** on the cutting mat. Mark a dot on the top edge 2" over from the upper right corner as shown. Align the diagonal edge of the 60° triangle ruler with the dot. The bottom edge of the ruler should be even with the bottom edges of the rectangles. Cut. Use all pieces in Step G.

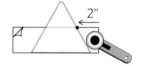

G. Stitch the Step C units between the Step F units as shown. Align raw edges exactly as shown in the photo. Press seams toward the white. Make 2.

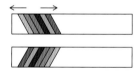

H. Stitch the white 1" × 2¼" rectangle to the print 1" × 9" strip. Press toward the print.

Stitch the resulting strip between the Step G rows, aligning the seam as shown. Press toward the center. The ends will not be even. Trim the unit to 4" × 9½".

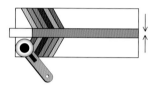

I. Stitch the Step E and Step H units together. Press away from the triangle. The block measures 12½" × 4".

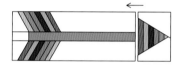

BORDER STRIPS

J. Stitch assorted white pieces together as desired for the length of the border strip in Step K.

K. Stitch a 3½" × 12½" strip to the bottom edge. Trim the block to 12½" wide × 6" tall.

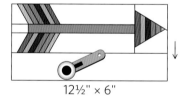

12½" × 6"

Sampler Assembly

It's time to gather together the blocks you've sewn and map out their placement.
Think of it like gathering memories in a scrapbook—but yours is made of fabric!
You'll be able to wrap up in it as you recall where you bought the fabrics, or perhaps
who you sewed them with—what fun!

✴ 62½" × 73½" FINISHED QUILT ✴

CUTTING

Assorted Prints

Enough 2½"-wide strips to total 285" in length for binding

SEWING

A. Stitch the Snowbirds row to the Red Arrow Highway block. Press seam away from the Red Arrow Highway.

B. Stitch assorted white pieces together as desired for the length of the border strip in Step C.

C. Stitch a white 3" × 43½" strip to the bottom of the Snowbirds/Red Arrow Highway section. Press seam toward the white strip. The section measures 43½" wide × 12" tall.

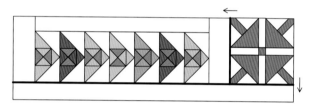

D. Stitch the Silicon Hills block above the Crosstown block. Press seam toward the Silicon Hills block. Section measures 15½" wide × 29½" tall.

E. Stitch the I Heart New York block to the Springfield block as shown. Press seam away from the heart block. Section measures 28½" wide × 20" tall.

F. Stitch the Hampton Roads block below the I Heart New York/Springfield section. Press seam away from the Hampton Roads block. Stitch the Silicon Hills/Crosstown section to the left edge; press. Section measures 43½" wide × 29½" tall.

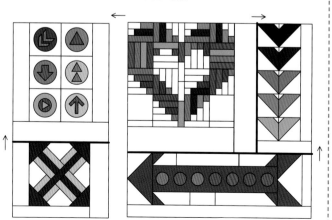

G. Stitch the Circle Pines, Spaghetti Junction, and Santa Fe blocks together to make a row. Press seams toward the center. Section measures 43½" wide × 15½" tall.

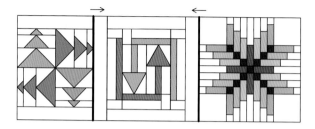

H. Stitch the Step C, F, and G sections and the Maui row together as shown. Press seams toward the top. Section measures 43½" wide × 66½" tall.

I. Stitch the San Francisco, Savannah Strings, Tennessee Two-Tone, and London Roads blocks together in a vertical row as shown. Press seams toward the top. Stitch this row to the Step H section. Press in the direction that looks best. Section measures 55½" wide × 66½" tall.

J. Stitch assorted 4" white strips together as desired to make borders long enough for the quilt. Trim two borders to the exact length of the quilt and stitch them to the side edges. Press seams toward the borders. Trim two borders to the exact width of the quilt and stitch them to the top and bottom edges. Press seams toward the borders.

K. Layer and quilt by hand or machine. Bind using 2½"-wide binding strips.

Blue Spruce Table Runner

When I see blue spruce trees, I remember a time driving through Colorado's Rocky Mountains. These tall, looming beauties were a sight to behold. It only seemed right to give them their own pattern.

✳ **FINISHED SIZE: 14" × 49"   FINISHED BLOCK: 8" × 10"** ✳

MATERIALS

Yardage is based on 42"-wide fabric.

- ⅝ yard of white print for block backgrounds
- 3—10" squares of assorted blue-green prints for trees
- 2—10" squares of assorted green prints for trees
- ½ yard of gray print for tree trunks, sashing, and border
- ⅓ yard of gray tone-on-tone for binding
- ¾ yard of fabric for backing
- 18" × 53" piece of batting

CUTTING

White Print

2—4" × 42" strips; from these strips, cut:
    10—4" × 4½" rectangles
    2—3" × 4" rectangles
    2—2" × 4½" rectangles
2—3" × 42" strips; from these strips, cut:
    10—3" × 4½" rectangles
    8—3" × 4" rectangles
1—2" × 42" strip; from this strip, cut:
    8—2" × 4½" rectangles

3 Blue-Green Prints

From *each* print, cut:
1—4" × 7½" rectangle
1—3" × 5½" rectangle
1—2" × 3½" rectangle

2 Green Prints

From *each* print, cut:
1—4" × 7½" rectangle
1—3" × 5½" rectangle
1—2" × 3½" rectangle

Gray Print

4—2¼" × 42" strips
2—1¾" × 42" strips; from these strips, cut:
    4—1¾" × 10½" strips
    Trim rest of strip to 1½" wide; then cut:
    5—1½" × 3" rectangles

Gray Tone-on-Tone

4—2¼" × 42" binding strips

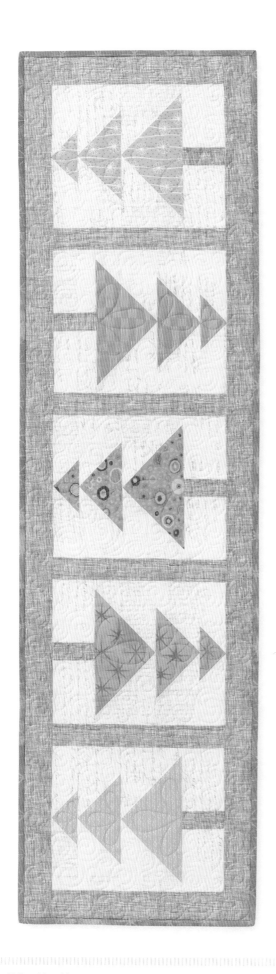

SEWING

A. Stitch two white 3" × 4" rectangles and one gray 1½" × 3" rectangle together to make a trunk unit. Press seams toward the center. Unit measures 3" × 8½". Make 5.

B. On the wrong side of a white 2" × 4½" rectangle, measure 2" down from the upper right corner and mark a dot. Mark a diagonal line from the upper left corner to the dot as shown.

Position the marked white rectangle on a blue-green 2" × 3½" rectangle with right sides together as shown. Stitch on the line.

✳ TERRY'S TIP
Mind the Crease

Instead of measuring and marking, place the background rectangle on top of the print and crease the edge as shown.

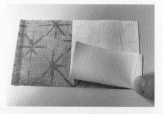

Mark a line on your machine straight out from the needle. Start with the needle down. Position the corner right up against the needle. As you stitch, watch the creased corner travel up the line.

Press toward the white. Trim seam allowance to ¼".

C. On the wrong side of a white 2" × 4½" rectangle, measure 2" up from the lower right corner and mark a dot. Mark a diagonal line from the dot to the lower left corner as shown.

Position the marked white rectangle on the print end of the Step B unit as shown. Stitch on the line.

Press toward the white. The edges should be straight and the point should be ¼" in from the edge. Trim seam allowance to ¼". Unit measures 2" × 8½".

D. Repeat Steps B and C using a matching 3" × 5½" rectangle and two white 3" × 4½" rectangles. Mark the dots 3" from the corner. Unit measures 3" × 8½".

E. Repeat Steps B and C using a matching print 4" × 7½" rectangle and two white 4" × 4½" rectangles. Mark the dots 4" from the corner. Unit measures 4" × 8½".

F. Stitch a trunk unit and C, D, and E units together as shown. Press seams in the direction that looks best. Block measures 8½" × 10½". Repeat Steps B–F to make one tree from each blue-green and green print for a total of five tree blocks.

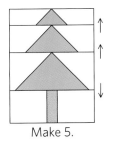

Make 5.

G. Arrange the five blocks in a row as shown, alternating the direction of the trees. Stitch gray 1¾" × 10½" strips in between the blocks. Press seams toward the gray.

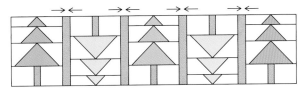

Stitch 2¼" × 42" gray print strips together to make borders long enough for the runner. Trim two borders to the exact length of the runner. Stitch them to the long edges. Press seams toward the border. Trim two 2¼" strips to the exact width of the runner and stitch them to the ends. Press seams toward the gray.

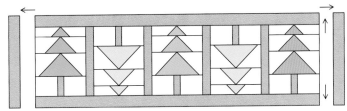

H. Layer and quilt by hand or machine. Bind using the gray tone-on-tone 2¼" × 42" strips.

Brooklyn Baby Quilt

Our son's college roommate and his wife live in Brooklyn, New York. They just had a baby boy, and I didn't finish his baby quilt until he was a few months old. I'm hoping baby Josh will soon have a little sister, because her quilt is actually ready!

✳ **FINISHED SIZE:** 46" × 44½" ✳

MATERIALS

Yardage is based on 42"-wide fabric.

- 1¾ yards solid white for heart background and border
- Assorted prints for heart: 1—5" × 21" strip, 1—3½" × 21" strip, and 10—2" × 21" strips (or use scraps for more variety)
- ⅛ yard of gray print for heart
- ½ yard of pink print for binding
- 3 yards of fabric for backing
- 52" × 52" piece of batting

CUTTING

White

4—10½" × 42" strips; from these strips, cut:
- 2—10½" × 36" strips
- 2—10½" × 34½" strips

1—6½" × 42" strip; from this strip, cut:
- 2—6½" × 8" rectangles
- 1—5" × 21" strip

1—3½" × 42" strip; from this strip, cut:
- 1—3½" × 21" strip
- 2—3½" × 3½" squares

2—2" × 42" strips; from these strips, cut:
- 1—2" × 21" strip
- 4—2" × 6½" strips
- 2—2" × 5" strips
- 2—2" × 3½" rectangles
- 4—2" × 2" squares

Assorted Prints

Cut 9 of the 2" × 21" strips into:
- 12—2" × 6½" strips
- 6—2" × 5" strips
- 3—2" × 3½" rectangles
- 6—2" × 2" squares

(*Hint:* Mix up the prints, cutting each size in a variety of prints!)

Gray Print

1—2" × 42" strip; from this strip, cut:
- 4—2" × 3½" rectangles
- 12—2" × 2" squares

Binding Fabric

5—2¼" × 42" binding strips

SEWING

A. Stitch strip sets as shown using the white and assorted print 21"-long strips. All strip sets measure 6½" × 21". Cut into 2" units.

✴ TERRY'S TIP
Stay on Track

Test your ¼" seam allowance before you begin. Stitch three 1½" × 3½" scraps together along the long edges. The resulting square must measure exactly 3½" × 3½".

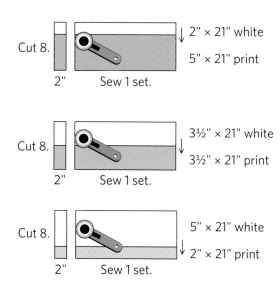

Cut 8.

2"

Sew 1 set.

2" × 21" white

5" × 21" print

Cut 8.

2"

Sew 1 set.

3½" × 21" white

3½" × 21" print

Cut 8.

2"

Sew 1 set.

5" × 21" white

2" × 21" print

B. Stitch Step A units and assorted print 2" × 6½" strips together to make 4 blocks **exactly as shown.** Press seams toward the 2" × 6½" print strips. Blocks measure 6½" × 6½".

Make 4.

C. Stitch Step A units and assorted print 2" × 6½" strips together to make 4 blocks exactly as shown. These blocks face the opposite way! Press seams toward the 2" × 6½" print strips. Blocks measure 6½" × 6½".

Make 4.

D. Stitch three assorted print 2" × 6½" strips together. Press all seams in the same direction. Unit measures 5" × 6½".

E. Stitch four assorted print 2" × 5" strips together. Press all seams in the same direction. Unit measures 5" × 6½".

F. Stitch a white 2" × 5" strip and gray 2" square together. Press seam toward the gray square. Unit measures 2" × 6½". Make 2.

Stitch a white 2" × 3½" rectangle, gray 2" square, and print 2" square together. Press seams toward the gray square. Unit measures 2" × 6½". Make 2.

Stitch a white 2" square, gray 2" square, and print 2" × 3½" rectangle together. Press seams toward the gray square. Unit measures 2" × 6½". Make 2.

Stitch a gray 2" square and print 2" × 5" strip together. Press seam toward the gray square. Unit measures 2" × 6½". Make 2.

Stitch the units together exactly as shown. Press seams all in the same direction. Blocks measure 6½" × 6½". Make 2.

Make 2.

G. Stitch a print 2" square and gray 2" × 3½" rectangle together. Press seam toward the gray rectangle. Unit measures 2" × 5". Make 2.

Stitch a gray 2" × 3½" rectangle and white 3½" square together. Press seam toward the gray rectangle. Unit measures 3½" × 5". Make 2.

Stitch a print 2" square, gray 2" square, and white 2" square together. Press seams toward the gray square. Unit measures 2" × 5". Make 2.

Stitch the units together exactly as shown to make two units. Press seams as shown by the arrows. Units measure 6½" × 5".

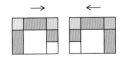

H. Arrange the blocks and units exactly as shown. Place white 6½" × 8" rectangles and 2" × 6½" strips along the bottom edge as shown.

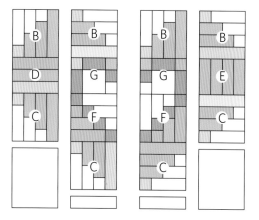

I. Arrange the remaining assorted print, gray, and white pieces to make a center row as shown. Stitch the units into rows. Press seams in opposite directions. Stitch the rows together. Press in the direction that looks best. The heart measures 26" wide × 24½" tall.

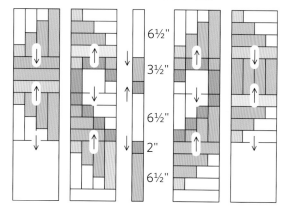

J. Stitch a white 10½" × 34½" strip to the right edge of the heart, stopping about 2" above the bottom edge. Press seam toward the white. **Pay attention!! The shorter strips are sewn to the side edges!**

Stitch a white 10½" × 36" strip to the top edge of the heart. Press seam toward the white. Stitch the remaining 10½" × 34½" strip to the left side of the heart and the remaining 10½" × 36" strip to the bottom edge. Press after each addition. Finish stitching the first seam. Press.

K. Layer and quilt by hand or machine. Bind using the pink 2¼" × 42" binding strips.

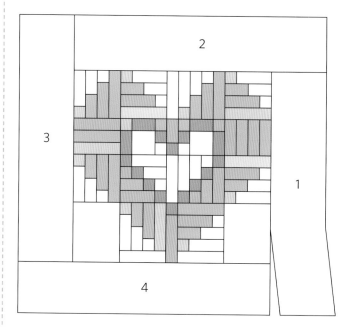

City Streets

When our kids were little we used to play a game in the car.
At each stop sign we would take turns choosing whether to go left,
right, or straight. It was a fun way to explore a new area. The kids
tried to get us lost, and the adults tried to get back on a main road.
We still do that when we're in a new city.

✳ **FINISHED SIZE: 51½" × 68½" (lap quilt shown)   FINISHED BLOCK: 8½" × 8½"** ✳

MATERIALS

Yardage is based on 42"-wide fabric.

	FAT QUARTERS (18" × 21") OF ASSORTED PRINTS*	BINDING FABRIC	BACKING FABRIC
Baby: 34½" × 43"	10	½ yard	1½ yards
Lap: 51½" × 68½"	24	⅝ yard	3¼ yards
Twin: 68½" × 94"	44	¾ yard	5⅔ yards
Queen: 85½" × 102½"	60	⅞ yard	7⅞ yards
King: 119½" × 119½"	98	1 yard	14¼ yards

* For more variety, scraps may be used.

OPTIONAL

A square ruler, 6" × 6" or larger, is handy for squaring up.

CUTTING

Assorted Prints

(*Hint:* No matter what size you are making, you will cut the same pieces from each fat quarter. All that changes is the number of fat quarters you are using.)

From *each* print, cut:
1—6" × 21" strip; from this strip, cut:
    2—6" × 6" squares
    2—4" × 4" squares
4—2" × 21" strips; from these strips, cut:
    4—2" × 9" strips
    4—2" × 6" strips
1—1½" × 21" strip; from this strip, cut:
    2—1½" × 9½" strips

Binding Fabric

Number of pieces for each size (baby, lap, twin, queen, king) is in parentheses.

(5, 7, 9, 11, 13)—2¼" × 42" binding strips

SEWING

Number of pieces for each size (baby, lap, twin, queen, king) is in parentheses.

Each print will be used for the background in two blocks and for the arrows in two blocks. For one block you'll need:

Background Print
1—6" × 6"
2—2" × 9"
2—2" × 6"
Arrow Print
1—4" × 4"
1—1½" × 9½"

A. Cut the background print 6" square in half diagonally. Matching centers, stitch the arrow print 1½" × 9½" strip between the two halves. Press seams away from the strip. Trim the square to 6" × 6".

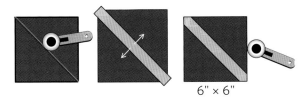

6" × 6"

✳ **TERRY'S TIP**
Straight Ahead

Stitch with the arrow strip on top to avoid stretching the diagonal edge of the background. When trimming the square, align the diagonal line on the ruler with the center of the strip.

B. Mark a diagonal line on the wrong side of the arrow print 4" × 4" square. Position the marked square on the corner of the trimmed Step A square with right sides together. Stitch on the line. Press toward the corner. Trim seam allowance to ¼".

C. Stitch background print 2" × 6" strips to the side edges of the square as shown. Press seams toward the background strips. Unit measures 6" × 9".

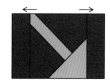

★ **TERRY'S TIP**

Right This Way

The arrow should point to the lower-right corner when stitching the strips to the side edges.

D. Stitch background print 2" × 9" strips to the top and bottom edges. Press seams toward the background strips. Block measures 9" × 9". Repeat to make (20, 48, 88, 120, 196) blocks.

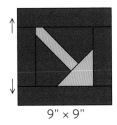

9" × 9"

E. Arrange the blocks in rows, rotating every other block a quarter turn as shown. Lap size is shown in diagram.

    Baby: 20 blocks set 4 × 5
    Lap: 48 blocks set 6 × 8 (shown)
    Twin: 88 blocks set 8 × 11
    Queen: 120 blocks set 10 × 12
    King: 196 blocks set 14 × 14

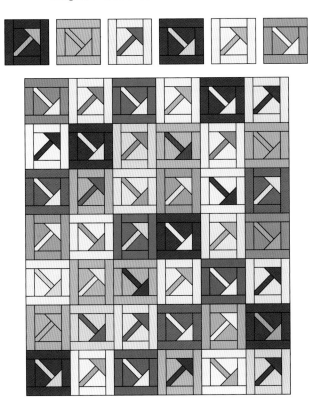

F. Stitch into rows. Press seams in opposite directions. Stitch the rows together. Press.

G. Layer and quilt by hand or machine. Bind using the 2¼" × 42" binding strips.

COLOR OPTION

For a more planned (and less scrappy) quilt, substitute the following fat quarters for the assorted prints listed in the materials chart on page 49. Use assorted lights for the backgrounds and assorted prints for the arrows.

	BACKGROUND FAT QUARTERS	ARROW FAT QUARTERS
Baby	7	2
Lap	16	5
Twin	30	9
Queen	40	12
King	66	20

Backgrounds

From *each* print, cut:

1—6" × 21" strip; from this strip, cut:
    3—6" × 6" squares
5—2" × 21" strips; from these strips, cut:
    6—2" × 9" strips
    6—2" × 6" strips

Arrow Prints

From *each* print, cut:

2—4" × 21" strips; from these strips, cut:
    10—4" × 4" squares
5—1½" × 21" strips; from these strips, cut:
    10—1½" × 9½" strips

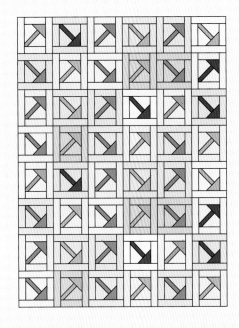

Turn Lane Table Runner

*Traffic can be frustrating, but it can also sometimes be inspiring—
at least for me! One afternoon while I was waiting at a red light,
I noticed that each car around me had a different-shaped turn signal.
I looked across the street, and there were more different turn signals.
The busy intersection paved the way for the Turn Lane Table Runner.
(At least something good came out of being stuck in rush hour!)*

✳ **FINISHED SIZE: 12½" × 36"** ✳

MATERIALS

Yardage is based on 42"-wide fabric.

- ¾ yard of tan print for block backgrounds and binding
- 5—⅛-yard pieces of bright prints for blocks
- ½ yard of fabric for backing
- 18" × 41" piece of batting
- Creative Grids 60° triangle ruler (8" size)

CUTTING

Tan Print

1—4½" × 42" strip; refer to diagram to cut this strip into:
    2—4½" × 8½" rectangles
    2—3½" × 7" rectangles
    2—2" × 7" strips

4½" × 8½"	4½" × 8½"	3½" × 7"	3½" × 7"	2" × 7"
				2" × 7"

2—3½" × 42" strips; from these strips, cut:
    18—3½" × 4" rectangles
2—2½" × 42" strips; from these strips, cut:
    16—2½" × 4½" rectangles
3—2¼" × 42" binding strips

3 Bright Prints

From *each* print, cut:
1—3½" × 12" strip; from this strip, cut:
    3 triangles using the 60° triangle ruler

2 Bright Prints

From *each* print, cut:
1—2½" × 21" strip; from this strip, cut:
    4—2½" × 4½" rectangles

SEWING

A. Layer two tan print 3½" × 4" rectangles wrong sides together on the cutting mat **with the long edge at the bottom**. Position the 60° triangle ruler on the layered triangles as shown below. The bottom edge of the ruler should be even with the long edge of the rectangles. The diagonal edge of the ruler should intersect with the upper left corner as shown. Trim. Discard the trimmed corner. Repeat with the remaining tan print rectangles. Trim 9 pairs.

B. Position a bright print 60° triangle with blunt end at the top and place a pair of tan print pieces as shown.

✳ TERRY'S TIP

Roundabout

We're using the triangle to trim the correct angle—no need to measure anything. Discard the trimmed corners. If you are left-handed, rotate the instructions and look at the diagram upside down.

Stitch first seam: With right sides together, the edges of the tan print piece should be even with both sides of the print triangle. Bottom edges intersect at the ¼" stitching line. Stitch. Press toward tan print.

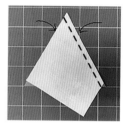

Do not trim the "dog ear" at the top.

Stitch second seam: Align the tan point with the little "dog ear" at the top. Bottom edges should intersect at the ¼" stitching line. Stitch. Press toward the tan. Make 9 units, 3 from each print. Trim units to 3½" × 7".

C. Stitch matching units together as shown. Press seams toward the top. Make 3. The joined rows should measure 7" × 9½".

Make 3.

Straight & Narrow

Straight, parallel lines of quilting are sometimes called matchstick quilting, especially when the lines are very close together. For the best results with straight-line quilting, attach a walking foot to your sewing machine. This foot moves the quilt top at the same rate as the quilt back, preventing drag and puckers. It's also best to stitch all of the lines in the same direction—from one side of the quilt to the other rather than using a back-and-forth motion.

Mark your lines before you begin, or use the inner or outer edge of the presser foot as your guide for consistent space between lines. You can also vary the width between lines for a different look. For wider space between lines than the presser foot allows, use a quilting guide bar or channel guide attachment.

D. Position a tan print 2½" × 4½" rectangle on each bright print 2½" × 4½" rectangle as shown, with right sides together. Mark a dot on the tan rectangle 2½" down from the corner exactly as shown. Stitch a diagonal line from the corner to the dot. Press toward the tan. Trim seam allowance to ¼". Make 8.

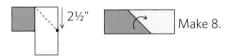

Repeat at the opposite end of each unit exactly as shown. Press toward the tan. The edges should be straight and the point should be ¼" in from the edge. Units measure 2½" × 8½". Make 8.

E. Stitch matching units together as shown. Press seams toward the top. Make 2. The joined rows should measure 8½" × 8½".

ASSEMBLY

F. Arrange the joined rows and remaining tan print rectangles as shown. Stitch the tan rectangles to the rows. Press seams toward the tan rectangles. Stitch the rows together and press in the direction that looks best.

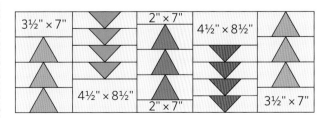

G. Layer and quilt by hand or machine. Bind using the tan print 2¼" × 42" strips.

Rectangle Rodeo

I love a fat-quarter quilt, and one of my favorite things when traveling is to visit local quilt shops and collect fat quarters along the way. When I cuddle up under the finished quilt, I enjoy memories of the places that I've been. The colors in this quilt were inspired by the denim and colorful shirts at a Kansas rodeo.

✳ **FINISHED SIZE: 54½" × 73" (lap quilt shown)   FINISHED BLOCK: 18" × 14½"** ✳

MATERIALS

Yardage is based on 42"-wide fabric.

	FAT QUARTERS (18" × 21") OF ASSORTED PRINTS	BINDING FABRIC	BACKING FABRIC
Baby: 54½" × 44"	9	½ yard	2⅞ yards
Lap: 54½" × 73"	15	⅝ yard	3½ yards
Twin: 72½" × 87½"	24	¾ yard	5⅓ yards
Queen: 90½" × 102"	35	⅞ yard	8¼ yards
King: 126½" × 116½"	56	1 yard	11¼ yards

CUTTING

Assorted Prints

(*Hint:* No matter what size you are making, you will cut the same pieces from each fat quarter. All that changes is the number of fat quarters you are using.)

From *each* print, cut:
2—4" × 21" strips; from these strips, cut:
    4—4" × 9½" rectangles
2—3½" × 21" strips; from these strips, cut:
    2—3½" × 12½" rectangles
    2—3½" × 6½" rectangles
1—2" × 18½" strip

Total Pieces

(*Hint:* For a very scrappy quilt, use scraps from your stash instead of fat quarters. The following are the total number of pieces you'll need to cut.)

	4" × 9½"	3½" × 12½"	3½" × 6½"	2" × 18½"
Baby	36	18	18	9
Lap	60	30	30	15
Twin	96	48	48	24
Queen	140	70	70	35
King	224	112	112	56

Binding Fabric

Number of pieces for each size (baby, lap, twin, queen, king) is in parentheses.

(6, 7, 9, 11, 13)—2¼" × 42" binding strips

SEWING

Number of pieces for each size (baby, lap, twin, queen, king) is in parentheses.

A. Stitch the 3½" × 6½" and 3½" × 12½" rectangles together as shown in a variety of combinations. Press seams toward the smaller rectangle. Make (18, 30, 48, 70, 112). Units measure 3½" × 18½".

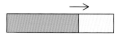

✷ TERRY'S TIP
Barrel of Fun

No need to worry about which prints are paired with each other, because they will all be touching in the final quilt. Try to mix up the prints and values as much as possible!

B. Stitch the Step A units together in pairs exactly as shown with the small rectangles at opposite ends. Make a variety of combinations. Press. Units measure 6½" × 18½". Make (9, 15, 24, 35, 56).

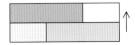

C. Stitch the 4" × 9½" print rectangles end to end in pairs as shown. Make a variety of combinations. Press. Units measure 4" × 18½". Make (18, 30, 48, 70, 112).

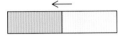

D. Stitch the Step B units between Step C units as shown. Press seams away from the center. Make (9, 15, 24, 35, 56). Blocks measure 13½" × 18½".

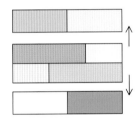

E. Stitch a 2" × 18½" strip to each block. Press seams toward the 2" strip. Blocks measure 18½" wide × 15" tall.

ASSEMBLY

F. Arrange the blocks in vertical rows as shown. Blocks in odd-numbered rows have the 2" strips at the bottom. Blocks in even-numbered rows have the 2" strips at the top.

> Baby: 9 blocks set 3 × 3
> Lap: 15 blocks set 3 × 5 (shown)
> Twin: 24 blocks set 4 × 6
> Queen: 35 blocks set 5 × 7
> King: 56 blocks set 7 × 8

✳ **TERRY'S TIP**
Map Your Route

If you'd like to have more control over color placement, stitch the 2" strips to the blocks **after** you have arranged them into rows.

G. Stitch the blocks together into vertical rows. Press seams toward the 2" strips.

H. Stitch the rows together. Press.

I. Layer and quilt by hand or machine. Bind using the 2¼" × 42" binding strips.

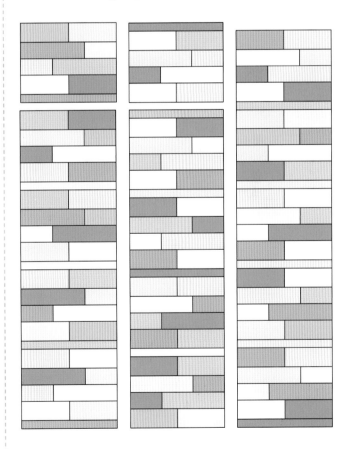

Travel Tote

I always like to have a project to work on while traveling, but I can never decide between knitting or hand sewing. Whichever I choose, this Travel Tote holds it all. Sometimes I even bring a tote for each.

✶ **FINISHED SIZE: 13¾" wide × 11¼" tall × 5" deep** ✶

MATERIALS

Yardage is based on 42"-wide fabric.

- ½ yard of main print for bag body (*Hint:* Use decorator weight fabrics for a sturdier bag or quilting cotton for a softer bag.)

- ¼ yard of polka dot for bag body (If your fabric is a one way print allow ½ yard in order to cut the print right side up.)

- ½ yard of solid black for accent strip and handles

- ⅝ yard of fabric for lining

- ¼ yard of fusible interfacing

- 22" × 30" piece of batting

- ¾" clip and D-Ring

CUTTING

Main Print
2—14" × 14" squares

Polka Dot
2—5" × 14" rectangles

Black
1—2¼" × 42" binding strip
2—2" × 29" strips
2—2" × 28" strips
2—1½" × 14" strips

Fusible Interfacing
4—1" × 28" strips

SEWING

A. Stitch a polka dot 5" × 14" rectangle, black 1½" × 14" strip, and main print 14" square together as shown. Press seams toward the black. Make 2. Stitch the two panels together as shown. Press the seam open. Panel measures 19½" × 27½".

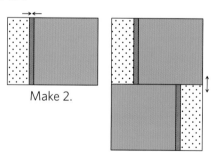

Make 2.

B. Cut batting and lining 2" larger than the panel. Layer the lining, batting, and fabric panel. Quilt by hand or machine. Trim the edges even with the fabric panel.

C. Fold the quilted panel in half as shown, wrong sides together. Stitch side seams using an ⅛" seam allowance. Backstitch at the beginning and end.

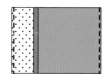

D. Turn the bag inside out and stitch ¼" side seams, backstitching at the beginning and end. These seams will enclose the raw edges.

E. With the bag still inside out, fold each bottom corner as shown. Mark a line perpendicular to the seam, 2½" from the corner as shown. Stitch on the line, backstitching at the beginning and end. This will make the bottom of the bag flat.

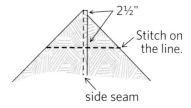

2½"

Stitch on the line.

side seam

F. Turn the bag right side out. Bind the top edge of the bag using the black 2¼" × 42" strip.

✱ **TERRY'S TIP**

Finish Line

Download free binding instructions at
AtkinsonDesigns.com/pages/how-to.

G. Matching centers, stitch each black 2" × 28" strip to a black 2" × 29" strip along the long edge using a ½" seam. The strips will be offset ½" at each end. Fuse an interfacing 1" × 28" strip next to the stitching line on the wrong side of each layer. Press seam open. Make 2.

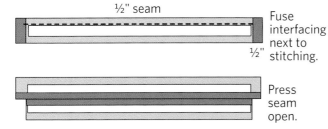

½" seam

½"

Fuse interfacing next to stitching.

Press seam open.

H. Fold the long raw edges over to meet the raw edge of the seam allowance and press. Fold the handle in half lengthwise and press. Fold the ends under ½" at each end to cover the raw edge. Press. Topstitch through all layers close to both long edges. Make 2.

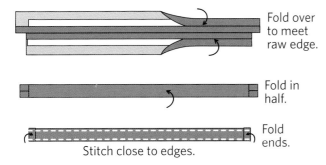

Fold over to meet raw edge.

Fold in half.

Fold ends.

Stitch close to edges.

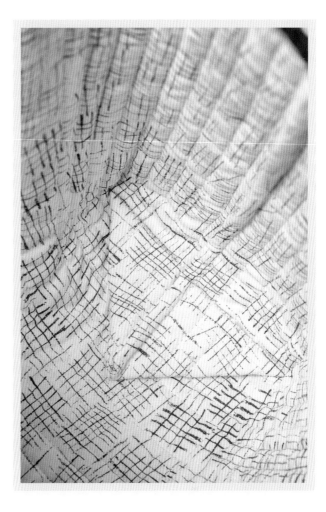

I. Position the end of one handle on top of the black strip, 2" down from the top edge. Stitch in place as shown. Change the bobbin thread to match the lining if desired. Fold the other end of the handle around the clip. Position it 2" down from the edge and stitch in place as shown. Repeat on the other side of the bag, using the D-Ring instead of the clip.

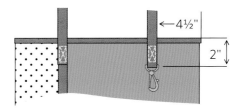

←4½"

2"

Zip 'n Go

Tuck tools and essentials into the Zip 'n Go bag and you'll have everything you need!

✷ **FINISHED SIZE:** 6½" wide × 1½" tall × 3" deep ✷

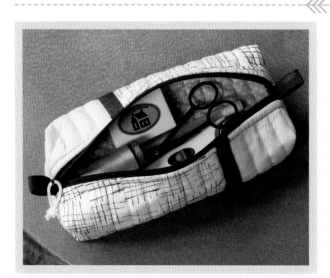

MATERIALS

Yardage is based on 42"-wide fabric.

- 1 fat eighth (9" × 21") of main print for bag body
- 1 fat eighth (9" × 21") of cream print for bag body
- 1—2½" × 21" strip of solid black for accent strip and loops
- 1 fat quarter (18" × 21") of fabric for lining
- 12" × 12" square of fusible fleece
- 14" zipper

CUTTING

Main Print
2—6½" × 5" rectangles

Cream Print
2—3½" × 5" rectangles

Black
1—1¾" × 10" strip
2—1" × 5" strips

Lining
1—11" × 11" square

Fusible Fleece
1—9½" × 10" rectangle

SEWING

A. Stitch a main print 6½" × 5" rectangle, black 1" × 5" strip, and cream 3½" × 5" rectangle together as shown. Press seams toward the black. Make 2. Stitch the two panels together as shown. Press the seam open. Panel measures 10" × 9½".

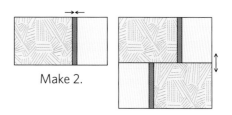

Make 2.

B. Center and fuse the fleece to the wrong side of the lining square. Layer the panel on top of the fleece. Use a walking foot to quilt straight lines or a darning foot to meander. Trim edges as needed to straighten the edges and square the corners.

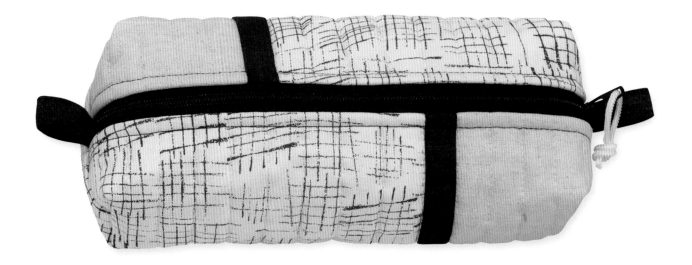

C. Press the black 1¾" × 10" strip in half lengthwise, wrong sides together. Unfold and press the raw edges in to meet at the center crease. Refold and press. Topstitch close to both edges. Cut 2—3" long units.

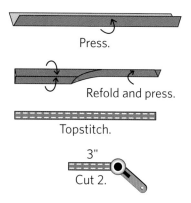

Press.

Refold and press.

Topstitch.

3"

Cut 2.

D. Fold each 3" unit in half to make a loop. Center a loop on the center seam of the quilted panel with raw edges even. Stitch a scant ¼" from the edge as shown, catching the loop in the stitching.

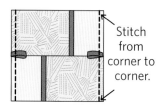

Stitch from corner to corner.

E. Align the zipper with the edge of the quilted panel, parallel with right sides together and edges even (zipper pull will face down). Stitch a ¼" seam through all layers. Zigzag along the seam to flatten the edge and prevent raveling.

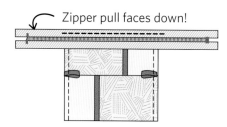

Zipper pull faces down!

F. Fold the quilted panel away from the zipper and topstitch a scant ¼" away from the fold, **making sure to catch the edge of the zipper tape underneath.**

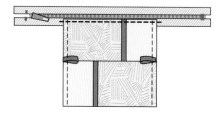

G. Fold the quilted panel in half and align the zipper tape with the opposite edge. Stitch a ¼" seam. Zigzag the edge.

raw edges even

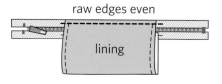

lining

H. Unzip the zipper and topstitch along the second half of the zipper (like in Step F).

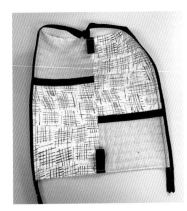

I. Close the zipper to make a tube. With the zipper centered, flatten the pouch and stitch a ¼" seam through all layers as shown.

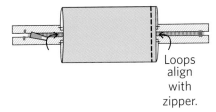

Loops align with zipper.

J. Unzip the zipper and stitch seam at the opposite end. **After stitching, make sure the zipper pull is between the seams.** Trim the zipper ends even with the fabric. Zigzag seams.

K. Fold each corner as shown and stitch a line ¾" from the point, perpendicular to the end seam.

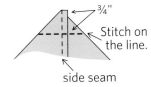

¾"

Stitch on the line.

side seam

L. Turn the bag right side out. Wiggle the ends to adjust the corners. Enjoy!

✳ **TERRY'S TIP**
Decorative Zipper Pull

Use an extra zipper to make a matching or contrasting pull for your zipper. Unzip and use just one side of the zipper. You'll need about 6"–7". Using sharp scissors, trim right next to the zipper coil (what would be called "teeth" on a metal zipper). Pull any loose threads away from the coil. Thread the trimmed coil through the zipper pull and tie the ends in an overhand knot. Trim the ends. Put a dot of clear-drying glue on the knot if desired.

Ribbon Road

This table runner was inspired by Colorado's Million Dollar Highway, which zigzags back and forth around switchbacks through the mountains between Silverton and Ouray. At each hairpin turn a spectacular view unfolds. It's hard to appreciate just how big the mountains are until you're looking down over the edge of a drop-off to a river far below.

✳ FINISHED SIZE: 14½" × 38½" ✳

MATERIALS

Yardage is based on 42"-wide fabric.

- 10—2½" × 42" strips *OR* 20—2½" × 21" strips of assorted prints for background (*Hint:* Use prints of a similar value and the "ribbon" will stand out more.)
- 1 fat quarter (18" × 21") of light red print for ribbon
- 1 fat eighth (9" × 21") of dark red print for ribbon
- ¼ yard of fabric *OR* use leftover strips for binding
- ½ yard of fabric for backing
- 18" × 42" piece of batting
- Pencil or chalk marker

CUTTING

Assorted Prints

(*Hint:* Mix up the prints, cutting each size in a variety of prints!)

8—2½" × 14½" strips
5—2½" × 10½" strips
10—2½" × 6½" strips
2—2½" × 4½" strips
2—2½" × 2½" squares

Light Red Print

4—2½" × 21" strips; from these strips, cut:
   29—2½" × 2½" squares

Dark Red Print

2—2½" × 10½" strips
2—2½" × 2½" squares

Binding Fabric

3—2½" × 42" binding strips

✳ TERRY'S TIP

On Your Mark, Get Set . . .

If you want to save time and mark your machine instead of the squares, refer to the general information on page 7.

SEWING

A. Using a pencil or chalk marker, mark a diagonal line on the wrong side of 20 light red 2½" squares.

B. Position a marked light red 2½" square on each end of four assorted print 2½" × 6½" strips as shown. Stitch on the line. Press toward the corner. Trim seams to ¼". Make 4.

Make 4.

C. Layer a marked light red 2½" square on top of an assorted print 2½" square with edges even and right sides together. Stitch on the line. Trim seam allowance to ¼". Press toward the light red. Repeat to make 2.

Make 2.

D. ROW 1: Arrange the Step B units in a row, rotating every other unit exactly as shown.

Place light red 2½" squares in between the units. Position a Step C square at each end as shown. Check to make sure the pieces are facing the correct way. Stitch together. Press seams toward the light red squares. Row measures 2½" × 38½".

Make 1.

E. Stitch a print 2½" × 10½" strip between two dark red 2½" × 10½" strips to make a strip set. Press seams toward dark red. Strip set measures 6½" × 10½". Cut into 4—2½"-wide units.

Cut 4.

2½" 1 Set

F. ROW 2: Make two rows as shown using one print 2½" × 4½" strip, two Step E units, two assorted print 2½" × 10½" strips, and one dark red 2½" square for each row. Press seams toward the dark red squares. Row measures 2½" × 38½".

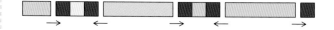

G. Position a marked light red 2½" square on each end of four assorted print 2½" × 14½" strips as shown. Stitch on the line. Press toward the corner. Trim seams to ¼". Make 4.

Make 4.

✳ TERRY'S TIP
Caution Ahead

Make sure this corner is facing in the correct direction before you trim the seam allowance. It's easy to get it backward! You may wish to arrange the rest of your rows to plan color placement before sewing.

H. Position a marked light red 2½" square on one end of a print 2½" × 6½" strip exactly as shown. Stitch, trim, and press. Make 2.

Make 2.

I. ROW 3: Make two rows as shown. Use two Step G units, one Step H unit, and two light red 2½" squares for each row. Press seams toward the light red squares. Row measures 2½" × 38½".

Make 2.

J. ROW 4: Make two rows as shown using two assorted print 2½" × 14½" strips and two assorted print 2½" × 6½" strips for each row. Press. Row measures 2½" × 40½". Make 2.

Make 2.

K. Arrange the rows as shown. Stitch the rows together. Trim the end of Row 4 even with the adjacent row. Press away from the triangles. The runner measures 14½" × 38½".

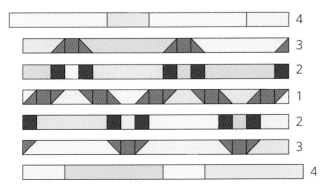

L. Layer and quilt by hand or machine. Bind using the 2½" binding strips or leftover print strips. You can download free binding instructions at https://atkinsondesigns.com/pages/how-to.

✳ TERRY'S TIP
Switchback Savvy

The rows below the center row are the same as the rows above, but they are turned to face in the opposite direction.

Evening Sky

Layered clouds float in the sky at dusk and everything
is peaceful. Break out the martini shaker and celebrate the
end of day with bright fruity drinks.

✴ **FINISHED SIZE: 63" × 71¾" (lap quilt shown)** ✴

TOOL

Creative Grids 60° triangle ruler (8" size)

CUTTING

Assorted Light Prints

From *each* print, cut:
4—4¼" × 21" strips

Choose (3, 5, 6, 7, 8) of the **total** strips. Cut them in half
to make (6, 10, 12, 14, 16)—4¼" × 10½" strips.

> ✴ **TERRY'S TIP**
> ## Getting Close
>
> Depending on the width of your fat quarters, these
> strips may not be exactly 21" long—no need to have
> an exact length. Square the ends of the strips,
> trimming the selvage off.

MATERIALS

*Yardage is based on 42"-wide fabric. Number of pieces for
each size (baby, lap, twin, full/queen, king) is in parentheses.*

	FAT QUARTERS (18" × 21") OF ASSORTED LIGHT PRINTS	GRAY PRINT	CORAL PRINT*	BINDING FABRIC	BACKING FABRIC
Baby: 63" × 41¾"	9	¼ yard	⅓ yard	½ yard	2⅔ yards
Lap: 63" × 71¾"	16	⅓ yard	½ yard	⅝ yard	3⅞ yards
Twin: 76" × 86¾"	25	½ yard	⅝ yard	⅔ yard	5⅓ yards
Full/Queen: 84" × 101¾"	29	½ yard	¾ yard	¾ yard	7⅔ yards
King: 120" × 120½"	50	¾ yard	1⅛ yards	1 yard	14¼ yards

* For more variety, scraps may be used.

Gray Print

(1, 2, 3, 3, 5)—4¼" × 42" strips; from these strips, cut:
(15, 27, 44, 52, 96) 2" × 4¼" rectangles

Coral Print

(2, 3, 4, 5, 8)—4¼" × 42" strips; from these strips, cut:
(18, 30, 48, 56, 96) triangles using 60° triangle ruler

Binding Fabric

(6, 8, 9, 10, 13)—2¼" × 42" binding strips

SEWING STEM ROWS

Number of pieces for each size (baby, lap, twin, full/queen, king) is in parentheses.

A. Stitch a gray 2" × 4¼" rectangle and light print 4¼" × 21" strip. Press seams toward the gray. Make (15, 27, 44, 52, 96).

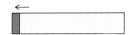

B. Stitch (3, 3, 4, 4, 6) Step A units together to make a stem row (baby/lap quilt is shown). Press seams toward the gray. No need to measure it because the length will be trimmed later. Make (5, 9, 11, 13, 16) stem rows.

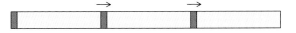

SEWING TRIANGLE ROWS

C. Trim Center Strips: Fold (2, 2, 3, 3, 5) of the remaining 4¼" × 21" assorted light print strips in half, wrong sides together, and trim as shown using the 60° triangle ruler.

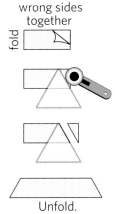

Unfold.

D. Trim End Strips: Layer a light print 4¼" × 10½" strip on top of a remaining light print 4¼" × 21" strip as shown with **right sides together.** Trim the end as shown using the 60° triangle ruler.

right sides together

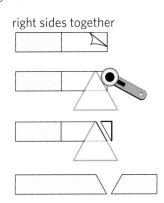

✳ TERRY'S TIP
Stop & Read!

Do not trim the fold! No need to measure anything, we're just using the ruler to trim the correct angle. Follow steps C–E and make one triangle row at a time so you can plan color placement and distribute prints evenly.

E. Stitch (3, 3, 4, 4, 6) coral triangles between the trimmed print strips to make a triangle row (baby/lap quilt is shown). See Terry's Tip below. Press seams away from the triangles.

Repeat steps C–E to make a total of (6, 10, 12, 14, 16) triangle rows.

✳ **TERRY'S TIP**
Down the Road

Position the coral triangle with the blunt end at the bottom. This will keep the straight grain along the edge of the strip.

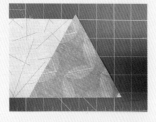

Stitch the first seam: Flip the coral triangle back onto the left-hand light print strip with right sides together. The blunt end of the triangle is at the bottom, and the top edges should intersect at the ¼" seam line. Stitch. Press seam away from the triangle.

Do not trim the "dog ear" at the bottom. No "dog ear"? Did you press away from the triangle?

Stitch the second seam: To add the right-hand light print strip, its point should align with the little "dog ear" at the bottom, and the top edges should intersect at the ¼" stitching line. Stitch. Press seam away from the triangle.

TRIMMING GUIDE ROW

F. Measure and trim the end of **one** stem row as shown. Discard the trimmed end. Mark this row with a safety pin. It will be the "guide row."

> Baby: 63"
> Lap: 63"
> Twin: 76"
> Full/Queen: 84"
> King: 120"

ASSEMBLY

G. Position a triangle row below the guide row. Slide it over to offset the triangles. Trim the ends even with the guide row. Position a second triangle row above the guide row, rotating it so the triangles face the opposite way. Slide it over to offset the triangles. Trim the ends even with the guide row. Matching centers and ends, pin and stitch the rows together. Press seams away from the triangles.

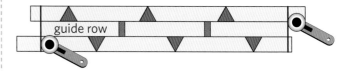

H. Position a stem row as shown and slide it over to offset the gray rectangles. Trim the end even. Stitch the trimmed piece to the opposite end of the row. Trim the row to match the length of the guide row. Matching centers and ends, pin and stitch the rows together. Press seams away from the triangles.

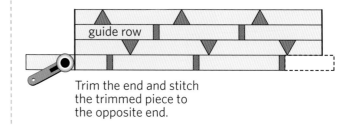

Trim the end and stitch the trimmed piece to the opposite end.

I. Continue to add rows in this manner, alternating stem rows and triangle rows. Remember to rotate every other triangle row. It's okay to add rows to the top or the bottom as needed to balance the colors. If you want to offset the triangle rows more than the length of the rows allow, trim the extra off one end and sew it to the opposite end of the row as you did in Step H with the stem row.

Baby: 11 rows
Lap: 19 rows (shown)
Twin: 23 rows
Full/Queen: 27 rows
King: 32 rows

J. Layer and quilt by hand or machine. Bind using the 2¼" × 42" binding strips.

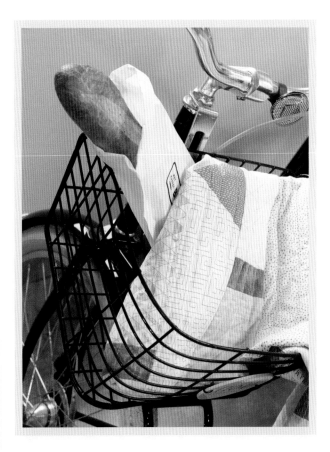

✳ **TERRY'S TIP**
Make the Way Easier

Trim each row to match the guide row **before** you stitch it to the quilt. **Use pins!!** This will keep the quilt from stretching and growing wider as you add the rows.

About the Author

Terry Atkinson lives in Elk River, Minnesota, and has been designing sewing and quilting patterns for over 20 years. When she's not getting creative and playing with fabric in her sewing room, you can find her exploring the great outdoors in her Airstream.

Watch "Terry's Tips" how-to videos at her website: AtkinsonDesigns.com

Acknowledgments

Many thanks to my husband, Kirk, who runs the business end of things at Atkinson Designs, and to my wonderful assistant, Greta Anderson, who is always ready to dive in and help whenever she is needed.